"...the breadth and depth of the readings are ⟨ here than one could use in any one semester, w very wide range of options. That's all one could

Northern ⟨irginia ⟨⟨⟨⟨⟨⟨⟨⟨⟨⟨⟨⟨⟨

"...placing the apparatus primarily in the first chapters and then leaving the anthology relatively apparatus-free (except for questions following the entries) is an excellent idea."

—Lois Feuer
California State University @ Dominguez Hills

"I see the value of this approach and it fits with my approach on 'critical thinking' skills that students can employ in a variety of situations."

—Shelly Dorsey
Pima Community College, Downtown Campus

"This book approaches the concepts behind writing from a workshop perspective. The reader feels involved in the process of discovering how to develop better writing skills."

—Alette Corley
Bethune-Cookman College

"What impressed me most was its practicality."

—Bridget Moss
Student Reviewer

"I like the thematic breakdown a great deal. . . . The categories are broad and general enough that these categories could also be applied to discussions of current issues and topics."

—Brenda Boudreau
McKendree College

"I am impressed by the greater emphasis on student's primary responses and on being aware of what they 'want' from the reading experience."

—Robert Lunday
Houston Community College/Southeast

"This is a well thought-out text... It has plentiful introductory and explanatory material, but not so much as to overwhelm the student."

—Keith Huneycutt
Florida Southern College

ACTING:
The GISTER Method

By

Joe Alberti, Ph. D.
In collaboration with Earle R. Gister

THE JOY PRESS
NEW YORK
2015

ISBN: 978-0-9727450-3-1

contents

CHAPTER 4 *How do I get what I want?* 63

CHAPTER 5 Putting it all Together 75

Act IV 77

Introduction

IN 1991 AT THE UNIVERSITY OF TEXAS AT DALLAS, Dr. Robert Corrigan was directing a student production of his translation of Anton Chekhov's *The Sea Gull*. The student cast struggled to come to terms with acting Chekhov. The challenge of developing Chekhovian characters and playing his subtext exposed many weaknesses in both our individual and collective approaches to performance. Sensing our dilemma, Corrigan invited Earle R. Gister, then Associate Dean and Master Acting Teacher of the Yale School of Drama to work with us by introducing his method of acting, which included a very specific set of principles that the actor could apply not just to Chekhov, but to all plays. After Gister left we applied the knowledge gained from the work with him to the production of *The Sea Gull*. The result was a performance that was not only lyrical, but also had greater resonance and meaning than we would have generated without Gister's help.

The following year, Gister returned to UTD and led another workshop, this time dealing with Strindberg. The methodology was the same, but he shifted emphasis from analyzing a play in order to discern humanistic elements in the writing to link character and action (as in Chekhov) to spiritual and supernatural elements that are inherent in Strindberg's writing, showing us how to realize those elements on stage. The next year, Gister again returned and offered a more advanced and altogether unique approach to training, using Samuel Beckett's plays that built on his foundational approach to Chekhov, Strindberg and other modern playwrights. The results of Gister's workshop on Beckett was even more powerful than the ones on Chekhov and Strindberg, as he introduced, taught, and demonstrated

1

an entirely new and higher level of technique, quite different from anything any of us had ever seen before, showing that indeed his methodology was applicable to more than the plays of Chekhov. In order to learn more about Gister's work, I attended the Yale School of Drama shortly after graduating from UTD.

Gister's work had never been formally written about. In 2004, I met with him at the Actors Center to discuss writing my doctoral dissertation about his acting methodology. He granted me full permission to do so. Since then, I have interviewed him many times, both about the historical evolution of his methodology and about his life. After completing my dissertation, *The Acting Methodology of Earle R. Gister; an Examination of Foundational Principles*, in collaboration with Gister, I wrote this book. Through this collaboration we hope to create and preserve a definitive reference on Gister's acting methodology.

Gister has been involved with actor training since the early 1960s, beginning his professional teaching career at Carnegie Mellon University and eventually heading its drama program, through 1975. He directed the Leonard Davis Center for Performing Arts at the City College of New York from 1975–1980 and was associate dean of the Yale School of Drama from 1980–1996. Gister was also the first chairman of the first panel of the National Endowment for the Arts. Some of his other notable contributions to theatre and theatre training include co-founding the League of Professional Theatre Training Programs, advising with the National Endowment for the Arts, and co-chairing the training panel of the Theatre Communications Group. Gister "played a significant role in nurturing and development of most of the major theatre training programs in the country" (*Playbill* 2005).

Influences

Constantine Stanislavski formalized a system of acting that has undergone many changes and adaptations over the last hundred years. Though it was formalized, he never intended his system to be a final treatise on acting. His work continually evolved up until his death, as he made many modifications to it over time, discarding or retaining approaches depending on their value in helping actors to produce effective stage acting. Those he kept, he would either use unchanged or build into even better theories. For example, his use of the objective was and is a powerful element in his system, so effective for the actor that it continues to serve the work of building character into the twenty-first century and is most often associated with his system. However, he discarded sense-memory late in his career, deciding that it distanced the actor from the imaginary circumstances of the play, because in sense-memory work the actor playing a given character would recall a private, historic event from his (the actor's) own past in order to evoke an emotion that may or may not be consistent with the playwright's intention for that character. Discarding theories that he felt were ineffective and retaining and building on theories that he felt showed promise was a style of working that Stanislavski adopted in his endeavor to create better and more effective approaches to acting.

Students of Stanislavski: Strasberg, Chekhov, Meisner et al:

Methods and techniques of acting have evolved since the introduction of the work of Constantine Stanislavski. He had many students who employed elements of his work, emphasizing certain aspects while ignoring or marginally incorporating others, making them the driving principles in their own pedagogies of actor training. For example, the work of Stanford Meisner was strongly communication-based. Lee Strasberg was particularly interested in emotional (affective) and sense-memory, despite the fact that Stanislavski abandoned them. Sonia Moore was largely interested in the *Method of Physical Actions*, as was Jerzy Grotowski. The work of Michael Chekhov, while retaining Stanislavski's use of the objective and super-objective, rejected emotional and sense-memory even before Stanislavski did, substituting use of the imagination rather than recollection as a means for the actor to enter into the emotional life of a character.

Gister

Earle Gister's methodology includes some techniques that can be traced to elements of the Stanislavski system, such as the super-objective and the objective while others, such as a unique definition of action that improves upon psychologically based traditional notions, can be traced to Paul Mann. Still other aspects of Gister's methodology, such as imagination rather than emotional and sense-memory (mentioned above) and image-based principles of physical transformation (characterization), can be traced to Michael Chekhov. However, Gister offers other unique and important ideas that can contribute greatly to the literature on acting theory. Not only has he adopted the best of some theories of acting while inventing others, but he has structured them all into a very clear, concise and effective methodology that can be recognized by his students as distinctly his own. In addition to a thorough analysis of the play through pragmatic concepts, Gister's work calls for a rigorous application of a series of questions designed to help the actor transform self into character and to design a structure that helps the actor, as the character, to take the journey from the beginning to the end of the play.

Plays are subject to many different interpretations, depending in large part on who is doing the interpreting. Plays in script form must undergo transformations in order to create a production. When a play is in rehearsal, there is a director, set designers, costume designers, and sound and lighting designers—all working toward getting the play ready for performance. The same is true of the actors. For the actors, the play starts out with the script. The actor must analyze the text with the goal of behaving truthfully and believably in the imaginary circumstances of the play. This concept is so simple that the actor sometimes overlooks it: plays are not "real life." Plays are about a playwright's view of events and the characters involved in them. Plays are about what it means to be human, including funny and painful moments, social and political issues, joy and sadness.

As an actor, you serve humanity in the playing of a role to the fullest of your ability. In order to do this, it is important to see how your character sees, hear how your character hears, and fulfill the needs of that role. It is often through an interaction of all of the characters that the tapestry of a play is woven: your character comes to be an important and necessary part of the whole. Philosophical and psychological examinations of a play, while interesting and revealing about the play's overall meaning, may get in your way when acting a part if the insights derived from them do not help you define who the character is, where and when he is, what he wants, and how you, as that character, choose and play affective action.

This book offers a clear and structured approach, beginning with a series of questions to help you to address elements necessary to define when playing a role: *Who am I?*, *Where am I?*, *When am I there?*, *What do I want?*, *How do I get what I want?*, and *What do I do if I get or fail to get what I want?* Although the process can be easy to understand intellectually, its application requires discipline and practice in order to understand it viscerally and use it fully in rehearsal and performance. The structure of this methodology is flexible enough to grant you the freedom to live and breathe spontaneously as the character within the given circumstances of the play.

Although directors, playwrights, and educators will benefit from this book, the main audience is "you" the actor, a talented artist dedicated to bringing a character to life for the audience each night. Throughout this book, the pronoun "you" will generally speak to the actor/reader, but invites readers from all areas of interest and expertise to examine the material and consider possibilities for each particular specialization. This book is designed to support you in making discoveries and to deepen yourself into the role without imposing a rigid and prescribed way of doing things. It starts with a series of questions, not answers. By working with the questions, discoveries can be made that will lead to choices and action. Once choices are made through addressing the questions, you can begin to play within that structure and make more discoveries and refine choices. This allows for the arousal of emotion with freshness at each and every performance. From this strong, foundational under-standing you can forget about yourself and make moments happen within the structure of the script, allowing the play to come alive as it was intended. This approach provides you with a foundation that can be repeated, so that what you do in your first performance of a role can be done in subsequent performances, without having to mimic what was previously done. Text analysis is a way to structure your work, so that you can play the play and have fun in the playing of it. It is the easiest and simplest way to overcome stage fright and indulgent acting.

The methodology is applicable to nearly any play, from the earliest Greek dramas through the modern periods. It is worth considering whether the methodology can be applied to flawed plays. Although a poorly written play will make it more difficult to answer *Who am I?*, *Where am I?*, and *When am I there?*, it is rare that a play will make it past the workshop stage if there is not a clear sense of *What do I want?* from each character. By answering these four questions, the actor can then make choices about the question *How do I get what I want?*. A poorly constructed play may offer the actor *more* possibilities to make interesting, vital choices and to take action that generates experiences in the realization of those choices. While this may be small compen-sation for being in a below-average play, it helps to see every role as a learning opportunity and a chance to take your craft to a new level.

Applying the methodology starts with analyzing the play. Read the play thoroughly at least three times in order to examine and understand it from three perspectives: 1) the plot and various plot lines, 2) the given circumstances or facts, and 3) the story from your character's point of view. Pay attention to what is going on with respect to your character. Jot down words or phrases as you read, noting what the play is about and considering what overall experience the play might be for the audience. Adopt a different point of view of the play than that of a critic or a set designer or a psychologist. Take your notes from the character's perspective. As time progresses, you will almost always come to understand the political and social implications of the play, but as an actor, it is most important that you understand what the events mean to the character and how the character contributes to the experience the play is meant to have on its audience. And now, let's begin!

Who am I?

*W*HO AM I? REFERS TO *YOU*, AS THE CHARACTER. THE question refers directly to the *identity* of the character and will always have a variety of answers. Usually there are basic facts outlined or implied by the playwright in character descriptions and/or revealed through the dialogue. This often includes a physical description along with the character's age. For example, in *A Fool for Love*, listen to Sam Shepard describe Eddie: "When he walks, he limps slightly and gives the impression he's rarely off a horse. There's a peculiar broken-down quality about his body in general, as though he's aged long before his time. He's in his late thirties" (Shepard 1983, 20). While the playwright may provide character descriptions such as this, you may not discover more subtle traits of the *Who am I?* (perhaps shyness, cynicism, deep-seated anger, a rhythm of walking, or spiritual habits) until you are on your feet in rehearsal, speaking the lines, moving through the blocking, and fulfilling your *action* choices that are connected to your *objective* choice. (You'll find out more about actions and objectives in the coming chapters.)

Often as an actor, you will continue to make discoveries about the *Who am I?* through reflective thinking off-stage and in your work during rehearsal and performance, as discoveries are typically made through doing. It is in this sense that the question *Who am I?* is ongoing. You may continue to make discoveries about the character long after the performance run is over. The *Who am I?* is a process of exploration; therefore, cultivating a mood of *openness* in your inquiry will help you with the discovery process.

The Play as a Guide to *Who am I?*

Begin the work of transformation into the *Who am I?* by carefully reading and re-reading the play. Initially, read the play from three perspectives.

First Reading

In your first read-through, allow yourself to simply read and experience the play. Become familiar with the entire play and all of its characters before analyzing the specific character you will be playing. Don't focus solely on your role and don't focus on your *Who am I?* (the character you will be playing). After letting the play wash over you in that first reading, ask yourself, *What is the play about?*, then begin to articulate specific answers. Actors are intuitive people. Your experience of the play during this first open reading may very well reveal to you the kind of audience experience intended by the playwright. This will clue you in tremendously in terms of playing the role. Boil down your thoughts on what the play is about to an essential statement or two that will focus on primary elements. You can always amend this statement or change your opinion as you go deeper into the play. This is simply a preliminary understanding to give you perspective into the world of the play.

For example:

- *Hamlet* by William Shakespeare is about *ambition, murder,* and *revenge.*
- *Hedda Gabler* by Henrik Ibsen is about *greed, jealousy,* and having a *meaningful purpose in life.*
- *Miss Julie* by August Strindberg is about *status as an obstacle to human potential.*
- *Race* by David Mamet is about *prejudice, perception,* and *lies.*

Second Reading

In the second read-through, separate fact from opinion. A fact can be proven. It is an assertion for which evidence is provided in the play. Look not only for facts about your character, but facts about the play as a whole as well. Often, you may find a fact that seemingly has little to do with your *Who am I?* turns out to matter greatly. Do not take what one character says about another character or even about themselves at face value or as the absolute truth. Characters, like real people, have agendas and reasons for saying what they say. Search for those facts that are bedrock, provable and, therefore, reliable. Those facts will serve as jumping-off points for addressing all of the major questions, beginning with *Who am I?*.

Example: *Miss Julie* by August Strindberg.

CHRISTINE: Well, Miss Julie, you have had fiancés yourself. (Fact)
JEAN: I'm not conceited. (Opinion)

Example: *Mother Courage* by Bertolt Brecht.

YVETTE: I left them here. (Fact)
MOTHER COURAGE: She's not a captivating young person. She's a respectable young person. (Opinion)

Example: *The Weir* by Conor McPherson.

VALERIE: I was brought into, a room and Niamh was on a table. It was a table for table tennis, and an ambulance man was giving her . . . the kiss of life. (Fact)
FINBAR: Ah, you're a terrible man, Brendan. (Opinion)

Example: *Cat on a Hot Tin Roof* by Tennessee Williams.

MARGARET: It's malignant and it's terminal. (Fact)
BRICK: you're foolin' with something that nobody oughta fool with. (Opinion)

Third Reading

In the third read-through, examine the play from the point of view of the *Who am I?*. Each character has a unique personal perspective, and, although he may share the same events of a given time and place with other characters, his perceptions may differ considerably. Each character has his own story within the play. Articulate this story as a narrative to yourself regarding your *Who am I?*. It is crucial to see and hear through the eyes and ears of the character as defined in the text. That means to create a narrative that reveals you as the *Who am I?*. Read for facts about yourself, as the character, (rather than the play in general, as in reading number two, although some facts may be pertinent) and your way of seeing the world. In playing Andre in *The Three Sisters*, for example, consider that, although the play is not called "*Andre* and his Three Sisters," you, as Andre, can look at the play in that way. Your narrative, as you work through your examination, might include something like this as a starting place:

> My name is Andre. I have three sisters. I was a university student in Moscow. Everyone says I'm going to be a professor. I speak four languages. I play the violin. I make things with my hands. My father died a year ago. I did not return to the University. I met a local girl named Natasha, fell in love with her, and asked her to marry me.

While your narrative should include facts drawn from the second reading of the play, it should also include opinions that you, the actor, formulate and make part of your *Who am I?*.

For example: I love my wife Natasha, and although I also liked her when we first started seeing each other (and through the first year of our marriage), I began to dislike her as time wore on. I discovered aspects of her personality that were distasteful to me. However, I have learned you can love someone and not like them very much.

Discovering distasteful aspects of Natasha's personality can occur for you (as Andre reveals in Act IV, calling her a "petty, blind, hairy animal . . . and not human") through a creative use of imagining the world from the point of you of your *Who am I?*.

If certain personality traits are not presented or implied, that may very well mean you do not need to define them and, therefore, need not search for their significance to your *Who am I?*. In beginning to address the question, it is crucial to use the pronoun "I" when referring to yourself *as* the character. For example, in playing Maggie in Tennessee Williams' *Cat on a Hot Tin Roof*, say, "I am married to Brick" and "I need to have a child." As Katurian in Martin McDonagh's *The Pillowman*, say, "I am a short-story writer" and "I have been arrested and am being interrogated, and I don't know why."

The question *Who am I?* should not be confused with a search for your own true identity. Addressing the question *Who am I?* is about playing the character as delineated by the playwright rather than making a given role about your own personality. It launches an investigation into the character as someone distinct from yourself. Playing of character, not displaying the actor's personal identity, is one of the most important virtues in the craft of acting. An actor playing the character Vanya (in Anton Chekhov's play *Uncle Vanya*) may determine that he should not aggressively pursue the character Yelena, with whom Vanya is in love, because it makes him (the actor) look desperate. In this case, the actor has made the role about himself and is concerned that he might look bad on stage. Vanya's character, as written, would pursue Yelena and do so in a desperate way. In fact, he steals morphine in order to commit suicide—in large part out of desperation—because Yelena has continually rejected him. In this case, the actor has failed to distinguish himself from the role because he refuses to allow himself to be seen as desperate.

Remember that a play is not about you personally, nor is it about your life and circumstances, though it may be about something to which you can personally relate. You could gain new insight into your life while analyzing your *Who am I?* in a play, but this might not happen each time. With the exception of trendy Hollywood stars, your audience does not care about your personal life, as far as your role in a play is concerned. Everything you do should be in service of the play and dictated by the needs of your *Who am I?*. Stage fright is sometimes heightened when an actor makes the role about himself, rather than about the character. If you are simply "being yourself" rather than playing the *Who am I?* and serving the play, self-consciousness can emerge, along with anxiety and tension, which will distract you from the role.

Preference for character acting is not unique to this approach. In *The End of Acting*, Richard Hornby notes that Stanislavski was a strong proponent for character acting, and we might all learn from Sir John Gielgud, who credited his accomplishment as an actor to the importance of discovering the character:

> *Of course, all acting should be character acting, but in those days I did not realize this . . . My own personality kept interfering, and I began to consider how I was looking, whether my walk was bad, how I was standing; my attention was continually distracted, and I could not keep inside the character I was trying to represent. In Trofimov [in Chekhov's The Cherry Orchard, with the Russian director Theodore Komisararjecsky] for the first time I looked in the glass [mirror] and thought, "I know how this man would speak and move and behave," and to my great surprise I found that I was able to keep that picture in my mind throughout the action, without my imagination deserting me for a moment, and to lose myself completely as my appearance and the circumstances of the play seemed to demand. (Hornby 1993, 86)*

This does not mean that plays do not seek to show circumstances that people will recognize as similar to their own. Who has not concerned himself with mortality, as Claudio does in Shakespeare's *Measure for Measure?*

> *The weariest and most loathed worldly life*
> *That age, ache, penury and imprisonment*

Can lay on nature is a paradise
To what we fear of death.

The Imagination

An essential way of addressing *Who am I?* is through active use of imagination. The imagination is your most important tool for entering into the given circumstances of the play and the life of the character. Like a muscle, the imagination needs to be exercised in order to develop. Practice using your imagination to create the necessary experience or image.

For example, if cast in *The Three Sisters*, an actor playing the role of the youngest sister, Irina, will discover that a love of romance is deeply connected to who she is. For the actor playing Irina, the use of imagination is of great importance in visualizing the man of your dreams. The more that you, as Irina, can create this "fantasy man" and all that life with him would entail, the more you will have a source for Irina's optimism in the first two acts and her breakdown in Act III when she realizes that her long-held dream will never become a reality.

Importantly, the more handsome and attractive you, as Irina, can make this dream man, the stronger source you will have for continuing to reject Tusenbach, who is in love with you and pursues you throughout the play. It is clear from the text that Tusenbach is unattractive. Having an image of a handsome man who will sweep you off of your feet is a crucially important source for the actor playing Irina. Beyond the romantic archetype, you, as Irina, should imagine the actual qualities that your fantasy man would have, ideally ones that are important to your *Who am I?* and, just as important, qualities that Tusenbach lacks. Moving beyond looks, this fantasy man might possess traits such as courage, loyalty, discipline, strength, and ambition.

Exercising Your Imagination

When you are in a play, you will be exercising your imagination daily through your work on the *Who am I?* and in addressing the other questions. When not in a play, set aside time daily for exercising and exploring your imagination, even if only for ten minutes. Like a muscle, your imagination will get stronger through use. Sit comfortably and picture a beach on a warm summer day. Imagine walking toward the lapping waves at water's edge, seeing the color of the sky and water, tasting the salt in the air, smelling the ocean, hearing the surf, and feeling the warmth and unevenness of the sand under foot. Taken further, read a play and let it stimulate your imagination.

You might read Anton Chekhov's *The Cherry Orchard* and imagine you are Gaev or Lyubov. Work your imagination by spending time with the specifics of the cherry trees outside a window of the house. Picture how you, as the *Who am I?*, used to play as a child among those trees. Recall a first kiss that took place in seclusion among the trees. Recall how your father used to walk with you and teach you about the trees and the history of the estate. Maybe your parents are buried out there. What else can you bring to mind to develop this scene in your imagination? Daily exercise on your imagination will prepare you for work on a role. Find ways to enjoy using your imagination, rather than making the work drudgery.

Transformation into Character

The first major step is to use the pronoun "I" when thinking and talking about your work on the *Who am I?*. Accept the negative aspects of your character, and do not allow them to distance you from the role. Do not make a judgment on the character based on your personal point of view. Labeling the character with a single word, or in a narrow way (good, bad, angry, jovial), often results in inhibiting exploration and leading to a one- or two-dimensional performance instead of pursuing the richness and fullness of another life on stage. From his own point of view, Richard III is not wrong for committing murder to achieve the throne. He is intellectually, physically, and emotionally driven to do so. In playing the role, obstacles you, as Richard, encounter to fulfilling your goal of becoming king should trigger negative emotional reactions within you, as the *Who am I?*. Even though you, as yourself, might not consider murder as a path to a goal, in the fullness of the moment and with the complexities of character the playwright, director (and you) create for him, your *Who am I?* as Richard III would consider murder a reasonable choice.

Be careful about assuming your character has knowledge early in the play that he would not have. You, the actor, always know more than the character knows, because you have the entire play before you. In playing Torvald, for example, you know that things won't work out for you and Nora, but Torvald does not know this until the end of *A Doll's House*. As Torvald, your confidence in a stable, permanent family life (you are so confident that you need not even question it) sets up the shocking revelation at the end of the play. This confidence is directly connected to your *Who am I?* and will inform your actions throughout the play. You must fore-go the knowledge that you, the actor, possess, and play each moment as if you do not know how things will unfold. This does not mean that characters assume they will always get what they want without concern for the future. There are obstacles along the way; otherwise, no drama. While some plays end with ". . . and they all lived happily ever after," others end with a question mark or weeping or bodies on the floor. It is important to make the distinction between what you, the actor, knows will happen and what you, the *Who am I?*, wishes, desires, hopes, or expects will happen.

Types

The majority of traditional Western plays are written with roles for three-dimensional, fictional characters. The playwright creates a world and inhabits it with "real" (realistic) people of his choosing. You may be able to draw upon interactions or observations of friends, family, and your life experiences to explore *Who am I?*. Many actors feel that playing a fictional character gives the greatest amount of freedom in a role and find it a gratifying and rewarding experience; one that takes little research and instead flows more or less naturally out of the actor's imagination through questioning. However, there are other types of characters you might encounter when cast in a play: stereotypes (often serving as functional characters) and real people.

Stereotypes and Functional Characters

In playing a role, you, as the actor, need to make the distinction as to whether you are playing a three-dimensional character, a stereotype or a functional character. A three-dimensional character is a unique persona, while a stereotype is drawn with a broader brush and has traits society recognizes as typical. Examples of stereotypes include a nerd, a sex goddess, a thug, a nutty professor, and a ditzy blond. If the character is written as a stereotype, it is necessary to identify and embody the traits of that stereotype. Ideally, you should transform to the point whereby an audience would recognize immediately that you are, for example, a romantic lover or an absent-minded genius. In order to successfully play stereotype characters you need to reveal the surface traits that make an audience member say, "Aha! He is a cad!" However, do not confuse a stereotype with a shallow personality. Also, keep in mind that a three-dimensional character might exhibit stereotypical behavior, such as feigning jealousy over a lover or a detective pulling out a magnifying glass and peering at a clue. The challenge is to develop that stereotype well without making it three-dimensional and changing the nature of that character.

Functional characters are in a play for the purpose of moving the story forward. You need to determine the character's specific purpose and how he supports the story. The messenger may be needed to give background on what has happened. The buffoon may serve to lighten tense moments. The butler may be needed to overhear an important plot point or simply to open doors and add dignity to the setting of a large estate. On the other hand, a butler such as Jeeves, brought to the stage from the stories of P. G. Wodehouse, is a well-defined individual and, therefore, a three-dimensional character. In fact, he is the star of the show. Three-dimensional characters need to be fleshed out by digging deeper than surface appearance, while stereotypes are depending on the surface appearance to fulfill their role in the play.

Ask yourself: *Am I three-dimensional; that is, am I a unique person or a stereotype or a functional character? If a stereotype, what specific stereotype? What do I need to do to transform myself into the stereotype? How do I need to transform so that the audience can recognize the* Who am I?*. If functional, how do I function in order to serve the play?*

Real People

Sometimes playwrights write about real people. Jeff Stetson writes about Martin Luther King Jr. and Malcolm X in *The Meeting*; Neils Bohr is central to *Copenhagen*; and Annie Sullivan unlocks Helen Keller's world in *The Miracle Worker*. For characters from recent history, find resources to draw on to help you transform into the *Who am I?*. The person may still be alive, and, if not, people who knew the person may be. Film footage, newspapers stories, audio recordings, and photos may be accessible. The good news is that if your character is well known enough to be featured in a play, he is probably well known enough to have been photographed and written about in other ways.

You may find that a few hours surfing the Internet is sufficient, or you may find yourself at the library or a museum or wandering through the neighborhood where your characters "live." For characters that existed before photography, such as Cleopatra and Mozart, there may be paintings and literature to use. The less historical background materials to draw on the more active your imagination must be. Sometimes people from history, such as President Richard Nixon, exhibit mannerisms that are instantly recognizable to an audience, providing you with a lexicon of physical mannerisms that you can begin to embody and express.

Ask yourself: *Am I based on a real person? Did the playwright intend for the role to represent or to stereotype the character? What resources are available to help me transform fully into the character?*

Anomalies

Through these repeated readings, your understanding of the character will deepen. If specific information is not found in the play, perhaps you do not need to investigate any further. However, at the same time, be careful not to dismiss missing information about your character as irrelevant. Remain sensitive to anomalies as well as inconsistencies in your early readings, because they often prove significant. In your early readings, look for the incongruity between what a character says and does.

If something doesn't seem "quite right" in your readings, look for the opposite of what you might think is true of your character. For example, in *The Cherry Orchard*, Lyubov receives telegrams from a man in Paris. She tears them up saying, "I'm through with Paris." However, she is in love with the man and later lets the cherry orchard be sold at auction and returns to Paris in order to be with him. Since you will have read the play through, you know her statement, "I'm through with Paris," is not what is in her heart. If you are cast in the play, use this knowledge to enrich your interpretation of Lyubov.

As you begin to make choices relevant to the character, events, and given circumstances, you will find times when there is ambiguity, and you will need to use your instincts and hunches in addressing *Who am I?*. In examining and playing the role of Natasha (Andre's wife), for example, note that at no time in *The Three Sisters* is any reference made to your having a family or friends. This is odd; an anomaly in a play that is in large part about family. The title is about family relationships. The very first line of the play refers to the sisters' father who died. Family relationships and family memories are referred to on almost every page. It is essential for you, as Natasha, to recognize that Chekhov never mentions Natasha's familial relations, although family references regarding the other characters abound. Recognizing that there is no mention of a family for Natasha, you might conclude it is because she has no family and, therefore, is driven to acquire one. This sets up the plot as she slowly takes over the entire house, dispossessing the sisters of their friends and home. For Natasha, the play ends with her possessing a home, two children, a husband, and, perhaps, a lover, while the sisters are outside, dispossessed of their home, destinies uncertain. You, as Natasha, can use the fact that Chekhov does not mention her family to make a strong character choice in determining that she wants one. You, as Natasha, can make a bold choice such as, "I am an orphan," directly addressing the question, *Who am I?*.

Although family is a crucial element in *The Three Sisters*, this does not mean it has equal importance in all plays. In *Waiting for Godot*, there is not much mention of family anywhere in the play, leading an astute actor to conclude it is not as significant in this play. You might spend copious amounts of time investigating what kind of family life the character Vladimir had or has without coming to any real conclusion.

The more you practice reading and seeing plays, the more adept you will be at finding the undercurrents and subtleties written in by the playwright. You will be able to limit time spent on unimportant details and have more time to examine the most vital aspects of the play.

Narratives

In that third reading, examine your *Who am I?* in order to understand his point of view on the world of the play. This point of view is strongly connected to the particular narratives of your character. Narratives are stories of individual and shared importance to which people (and, therefore, characters) not only relate, but allow to become deeply entrenched within them. As people, we share narratives about our personal lives, cultures, and professional identities—every facet of our lives. As an actor, work to identify your own personal narrative, often adopted subconsciously from your family and environment, which is driving your life. Through this exploration, you may begin to distinguish how you both connect with and differ from the character whose goals, ambitions, and life you will portray.

Narratives form the background; the often unspoken commitments that a community shares and out of which behavior arises. People (and characters) continually juggle the conflicts between their personal, family, and community narratives. Consider the importance of the local high school football team to a small town in Texas; in a distinct way, the identity of the town is, in part, defined by the team. When the team loses, townspeople feel they have lost something or fallen in the eyes of their neighbors. When the quarterback makes a great play, everyone feels like a better person. Narratives can provide strong sources for understanding the *Who am I?*. Through questioning the narratives to which a character and the world of the play belong, you will launch an inquiry that can lead to important discoveries that define your *Who am I?*.

The readings of the play will reveal elemental areas in the world of the play. Look to these areas as you investigate and address shared and individual narratives of the *Who am I?*. Within the narrative are values, beliefs, and truths. Importantly, these narratives evolve historically and out of traditions. On a simple level, ask yourself, *"What does it mean to be a middle-class man in 1890 in Europe?"*, if you have been cast as Torvald in *A Doll's House*. *"How do I view women and the role of the wife in the household in such a society?"* *"What would I expect in the way of behavior from my wife?"* In playing Torvald, begin with the pronoun "I," such as, "I see women as weak-willed and needing constant supervision when it comes to finance, social behavior, and political savvy."

On a personal narrative level, how do you see Nora? What is unique about her to you? Although calling her your "little song-bird" comes out of a larger view of how men at that time saw women, what is personally meaningful to you, as the *Who am I?* about Nora? Perhaps, "My little song-bird Nora is the prettiest wife among all the wives in our social circle."

When encountering the shared narrative among a group of people, recognize, for example, that citizens of the United States generally share a great respect for personal freedom. They dislike restriction, especially by overarching authority figures such as "the government." "Pulling yourself up by your own bootstraps" is seen as a positive character trait, and an independent woman might be proud of that fact, rather than worried that the neighbors would see her as "getting above herself" or being "masculine." In the narrative of a woman in 1850's Japan, barely able to get around on her bound feet, this "bootstrap" attitude would be unflattering, unfeminine, and undesirable. These shared narratives inform our identities, even if we are not aware of them. They shape the background from which we view and interact with one another in the world. Playwrights are informed by the narrative dynamic, which affects their writing and invention of characters and stories.

Once you identify important areas, begin to explore them in terms of the specific narratives that define them. Then begin to look at your *Who am I?* in terms of them. If playing John Proctor in *The Crucible*, ask yourself what it meant to be a farmer in Salem, Massachusetts, in the 1690s. Among other things, it meant great hardship, dependency on friendship and family for survival, belief in God and goodness, and a keen awareness of the presence of the devil and evil; for many people at that time and place, the devil, evil, and witchcraft were constant threats. Evil was real for them, and they could "see" it in "possessed" people. This was part of the narrative of the people; to play a character in *The Crucible* means incorporating that narrative into your *Who am I?*. Even if your *Who am I?* does not believe in the existence of the devil, you, as the *Who am I?*, are still part of that narrative and need to examine what it means to your *Who am I?*, if only, as the *Who am I?,* to deny it.

Passions

The character's passions are the most important areas to investigate when addressing the question *Who am I?*. Formulate this, too, as a question in terms of what the character likes, dislikes, loves, and hates, which are crucially important to address, because they go a long way toward answering the question, *Who am I?*. Our particular likes, dislikes, loves, and hates help define us as individuals, and it is also true of characters. Defining the particular passions of your character will begin to make your *Who am I?* distinct from others.

The investigation into the character's passions begins with the play. When you scan the play for facts you may discover through the dialogue that your *Who am I?* has certain likes and dislikes. You will also make more subtle discoveries when you read the play from the point of view of the *Who am I?*. These may not be "facts" but may be implied by and through what the character says and does. When you begin to see the world as the character sees it, the passions will become increasingly apparent to you. They need not be profound. They can be simple, yet meaningful to the character.

In *The Three Sisters*, Natasha likes the color green. This is evident because in Act I she wears a green sash with her dress. The oldest sister Olga points out that it doesn't go with what she is wearing, yet she still chose it. Natasha wants to make a positive impression on the family, and she wants Andre to ask her to marry him. It is perfectly in keeping with her *Who am I?* that she would dress in her best clothing and what she thinks looks best on her in preparation for her visit. She likes the color green and deliberately chose to wear the green sash. It is meaningful to her to the point whereby she is vulnerable to Olga's comment about the color not working with what she is wearing. Later, Natasha, having taken ownership of the house, makes a similar remark about Olga's clothing. Is this her way of getting back at Olga for her comment in Act I? If so, it reveals that she was stung by Olga's earlier remark, which implies that Natasha attached meaning to her green sash. If nothing else, it reflects that her decision to wear the green sash came as a preference for what she likes and believes looks good on her. Olga stating that the sash doesn't go with what she is wearing is taken in a negative way by Natasha, although none of this is spoken outright in the play. You, as Natasha, should take Olga's comment in this way: as an insult, although the situation would keep you from responding to her in a negative way, because at this particular time and in this particular place (the importance of time and place will be examined in later chapters), she has no choice but to accept Olga's comment. However, though Natasha behaves submissively in Act I, she is determined to have what she ends up having in Act IV.

Other times, what a character is passionate about is spoken directly through the dialogue. Listen to Beatrice and Benedict in Shakespeare's *Much Ado About Nothing*:

BEATRICE: You have stayed me in a happy hour: I was about to protest I loved you.

BENEDICK: And do it with all thy heart.

BEATRICE: I love you with so much of my heart that none is left to protest.

Not a lot of mystery here: Beatrice is revealing her passion directly to the source, Benedict. Simply put, she loves Benedict with all of her heart and tells him so. How important is that to the *Who am I?*. It is deeply important and informs her behavior on many levels.

When the likes, dislikes, loves, and hates are not obvious, examine the play for what is implied by the lines. For example, listen to Abigail and Proctor in *The Crucible* by Arthur Miller:

ABIGAIL: I know you clutched my back behind your house and sweated like a stallion whenever I come near! Or did I dream that? It's she put me out, you cannot pretend it were you. I saw your face when she put me out, and you loved me then and you do now!

PROCTOR: That's a wild thing to say—

You, as John Proctor, must make a choice in terms of whether or not you love Abigail. Your sensitivity, as an actor, to interpreting his responses to her will reveal that his feelings run deep, although he does not voice them. Making the choice that you, as Proctor, are in love with Abigail is in keeping with the play, for if it were easy to reject her, much of the tension implicit in the writing would be negated. You, as Proctor, should determine specifically what degree and kind of love you have for Abigail. Are you infatuated or deeply in love with her? How do you feel about your wife, Elizabeth? Do you love her? If you love them both, what are the differences in the ways in which you love them? Choices here are vital because they will inform the ways in which you relate to both women, the ways you perceive them, your thoughts about the future, and more. It is through your imagination that you can make your feelings of love for Abigail personal and immediate, thus aligning your physical, emotional, and mental self with the *Who am I?* (John Proctor).

As you investigate the *Who am I?*, note answers to yourself, even if some answers are just hunches. Once you begin to get hunches about your character's passions, you can begin to align with them. As Theseus in the beginning of *A Midsummer Night's Dream*, perhaps you recognize the kind of passion Lysander has for Hermia, although, being Duke of Athens, for political reasons, you support Egeus in forcing Hermia to submit to Demetrius. Perhaps a part of you likes and sides with Lysander, as you recognize that the passion he expresses for Hermia is an echo of yours for Hippolyta. Seek out hints, implications, and outright statements in the text regarding the likes, dislikes, loves, and hates of your *Who am I?*. Once you have explored the passions of your character, and they are resonating in you, hone in more specifically on the many other areas that will bring your *Who am I?* fully to life.

Other Areas to Investigate

In addition to passions, other fundamental areas to examine when addressing the *Who am I?* include your character's physical *body* and your character's *relationships*. Develop sensitivity to recognizing those areas that need exploration in a given play and define them in terms of the *Who am I?*. While certain areas may not be particularly important to address in some plays and with some characters; in others, they will be. For example, under relationships, political leanings are not nearly so significant in *The Zoo Story* by Edward Albee as they are in *The Enemy of the People* by Henrik Ibsen.

Offered here are examples of important areas and questions to ask in order to begin an inquiry. Each play will have its own specific areas for importance, so think of this not as a comprehensive list, but as a set of beginning guidelines, which you can adapt by adding and setting aside categories, according to the needs of each role. It is hoped that the examples and questions provide you with a model, so that when you are cast in a play you will be sensitive to identifying areas of importance, asking questions that lead to specific answers, and making strong choices on behalf of the *Who am I?*. Note that only simple suggestions are made for questioning a given area. It is trusted that you will take your work far beyond the examples provided.

Body

In examining the question *Who am I?* the physicality of the character must be considered. Through defining a few almost universal areas and practicing your examination and incorporation of them into the *Who am I?*, you will develop the skills for recognizing, defining, and incorporating another's traits of physicality when you identify them through reading and exploring the play.

Age

Age matters. A character's age is often defined by a playwright, either by being mentioned in the dialogue or noted in the character list. Sometimes it is necessary to determine a character's age by deduction. If significant time passes in the play, a character will age as well. If the age of a character is nowhere to be found in the script, then knowing the exact age may not be vital to the play. At that point, you might make a reasonable and specific choice through your imagination.

Ask yourself: *How old (either exactly or approximately) am I at the start of the play? Does my age change measurably over the course of the play, and, if so, does my behavior change as a consequence of growing older? Do I, the actor, need to make modifications in my walk, speech, or manner, in order to see through the eyes of the character at this age?*

Movement

If called upon to play someone older or younger, consider how age affects flexibility, movement, and physical expressiveness. If you are playing a stereotype, and it is clear that the playwright has deliberately written a two-dimensional character, consider that stereotypes are stereotypes because they are recognizable by an audience today. Therefore, how might the role require you to change your physicality in some way(s) that an audience would recognize?

Ask yourself: *If I were to do a physical gesture that stands for myself, as a whole, what would it be? Can I simplify the gesture? Is there a recognizable rhythm or pattern in my use of language (the lines) that might suggest a way of moving, as well? Might my hand have a tremor? Might I skip rather than walk sedately? Do I peer intently or move closer to a beloved child to get a good look at the face?*

Voice

Sometimes it is enough to use your natural voice and dialect; other times the play requires you to change them. Playwrights write dialogue with much forethought. These penned lines may differ from your rhythm, dialect, speech patterns, and word choices. Such differences might require you to organize your breathing differently. In all plays, especially classic texts, it is crucial to have the necessary breath support to fulfill the demands of the role. You must explore breath as a source of sound. You will compensate for lack of breath support through muscular tension. If you are asking your body to speak, but not giving it the fuel (breath) it needs in order to do so, tension will be the result.

Ask yourself: *Has the playwright indicated a specific dialect for me? Is there a recognizable vocal rhythm or pattern indicated or suggested in the lines? How can I organize my breathing to support the demands of speaking the text?*

Challenges, Disorders, and Illnesses

Playwrights write about universal issues concerning people. Sometimes these issues include characters dealing with physical and mental challenges. Recognize what the issue is, define it, and begin to embody and incorporate it into your work.

Ask yourself: *What is the challenge, disorder, or illness? Is it mild or strong? What information about it is given in the play? What research do*

I need to do (if any) in order to understand my challenge more fully? How does it manifest in my behavior? Does it get worse in certain circumstances or over time? A nervous tic will almost always become more pronounced in a tense situation. Stuttering may lessen when speaking poetry or singing.

Mannerisms and Habits

Playwrights may clearly indicate that a character has a mannerism or habit that you must incorporate into your work on the role. As a particular character, you may find that adopting a mannerism or habit is a useful way of expressing the character, even if the playwright has not specifically written this trait into the play. As an aging "player," perhaps you flip your hair back when talking. As a person with a guilty secret, perhaps you frequently touch your lips. As a young person with "places to go and people to see," perhaps you snap your fingers and tap your foot constantly.

Ask yourself: *Are there specific references or implications in the play about my habits and/or mannerisms? If there are no references, could a mannerism or habit add to your expression of the character as written?*

Emotion, Posture and Physical Expression

A depressed character will telegraph this state of mind through posture. It is difficult for a depressed person to remain upright, with an open, wide chest and a full smile. Conversely, it is difficult to be optimistic and cheerful with a sunken chest and a frown. Here are a few examples of how emotion manifests physically: Physical manifestations of resentment can include tightness in the body, especially the jaw. Physical manifestations of grieving, sadness and despair can include a feeling of heaviness, diminished energy levels, and a voice that lacks energy. Physical manifestations of anxiety can include shallow breathing, excessive movement and shrinking into oneself. Physical manifestations of a desire to achieve can include a lengthening through the spine and openess through the chest, and so on. Well-considered posture can intensify the *Who am I?*. It may be that no posture modifications are necessary as long as you are using yourself in service of the role.

Ask yourself: *Does my age require a physical modification of my usual way of standing? Are there physical traits or conditions indicated in the script and, if so, what adjustment(s) do I need to make in order to embody them? Is there any significant postural adjustments I could make in order* to more fully embody the character? How might my moods be observed in my posture, including the way I move in space and hold my face?

Relationships

The way in which other people see us can have a strong effect on our behavior. In addition to family relationships, a play might include relationships between friends, co-workers, school-mates, and associates in varying degrees of intimacy. Unless you are doing a one-person show, character relationships will always be a part of a play and must be investigated to determine what significance (if any) they have. Even a one-person show requires creating a relationship with topics in the play and the audience. We are social beings. It is in a social context that our identities have meaning and expression. Who we are is in large part a social construct through interaction. The ways in which we see ourselves in relation to others and the way they see us have a significant impact on the *Who am I?*.

Keep in mind that identity is not fixed but flexible. Consider that you, the actor, may not be the same person you are with your parents that you are with friends. When considering Irina's relationships in *The Three Sisters*, for example, it is important to define what her siblings Masha, Olga, and Andre mean to her. How is Irina's relationship with Olga different from her relationships with Masha and Andre? For Andre, consider that he, too, has a different *Who am I?* when he is with Olga than with Irina, than with Masha, than with Anfisa, than with Natasha, than with Sophie (and those are just with the women in his life!). To be even more specific with defining your *Who am I?* in a play, ask *Who are you to me?* and *Who am I to you?* in reference to the other characters. Being specific about these difference can help you to understand your *Who am I?*. If specific relationships are not mentioned in the play, perhaps they do not need further examination. However, if a relationship is brought forward in the play then it is important to question and define it.

Ask yourself: Who am I? *in reference to the other characters in the play? Be specific in defining this. Then ask: Who am I when I am with you? What does family mean to me? How do the others in the play see me? Which parent do I love the most? Am I from a large family or am I an only child? Do I have younger siblings? Older siblings? Am I married? Divorced? Never been married? Do I have children and, if so, who are they specifically?*

Status

Status is important in nearly all plays. A contemporary example of status might include a play set in an office, with a CEO, managers, supervisors, clerks, and janitors. There is often leeway in a modern status situation, and characters might communicate and interact freely up and down the chain of command or even ignore it entirely. An observer might not be able to determine "the boss" merely by observing an interaction. However, in Elizabethan England, status and behavior were more clearly and rigidly defined. A servant would behave specifically in the presence of a king, so much so that the behavior would be clearly recognizable. In a play written or set during that time period, status typically determines relationship behavior, even if it is in subtle ways. Consider the relationship between Hamlet and Horatio. Although they are friends and attended college together, there are many indications in their dialogue with one another that Hamlet is of a much higher status than his best friend, particularly in the way that Horatio addresses Hamlet:

HORATIO: Hail to your lordship!
HAMLET: I am glad to see you well: Horatio—or I do forget myself.
HORATIO: The same, my lord, and your poor servant ever.
HAMLET: Sir, my good friend, I'll change that name with you.

Differences in status can affect more than just how one character addresses another character in the dialogue. The *Who am I?* may be profoundly affected by status, or differences in status, within a play. One of the last scenes in *The Cherry Orchard* takes place between Varya and Lopahin. During the time period of the first three and much of the fourth acts of the play, there are references to the observation that Varya and Lopahin are a perfect couple that should be married. These references and observations are made not only by other characters, but by Varya and Lopahin themselves. In the final scene between Varya and Lopahin, the cherry orchard has been sold. Lopahin purchased it as it was sold at auction to pay the mortgage. Despite all of the talk that the two should marry, it is clear by late in Act IV that Varya is still waiting and hoping he will propose to her. During the day that everyone is planning to vacate the house, Lopahin is "around" the estate. There is a brief period of time when Varya and Lopahin are alone on stage. It is obviously *the* time for Lopahin to propose, based on all that has been building between them throughout the previous acts.

There is a long pause in their dialogue—a pause in which both characters are aware of the implications between them. Suddenly someone calls Lopahin from off-stage. He runs off as Varya slowly sinks to her knees on the floor. The audience's anticipation at the beginning of the scene that the two will become engaged by the end is not realized. Initially, Lopahin is alone waiting for Varya, so that he can propose to her. At the end, Varya is alone on the floor crying. From the audience's point of view the scene started with the prospect that finally the two characters would unite and ended with the realization that they never will. The characters, too, believed they would be engaged by the end of the scene. What went wrong?

In examining the scene, observe that it begins one way and ends in another. Discovering that it ends in the way that it does is crucial to understanding the characters. Careful analysis reveals that, although she takes an active role as a servant in the house, Varya is the adopted daughter of Lyubov, the owner of the cherry orchard. Therefore, she is of higher status than Lopahin, who grew up as a peasant. Despite the fact that Lopahin has been smart in business and has made enough money to actually purchase the cherry orchard, he still thinks of himself as a peasant, as he explains to Dunyasha in Act I. To Lopahin, Varya is on a higher social level than he, due to her relationship with Lyubov. Thus, despite Varya's desire and willingness to marry Lopahin, her status becomes an unspoken obstacle to Lopahin's proposal to her. Adopting the idea that scenes begin one way and end in another way gives you a means of framing and focusing an analysis on what happens over a given period of time and why it happens in order to reach meaningful conclusions. These conclusions can be the basis on which the actor makes interesting, vital, and appropriate choices on behalf of the character in terms of status.

Ask yourself: *Is status an important element in the play? Are there clearly defined levels of being in the play, such as king, queen, lady-in-waiting, and commoner? Are the levels less clear, but still giving indications of high versus low status? What dictates status in the world of the play? If the characters in the play were to line up from highest to lowest, how would the characters be ordered? Am I of higher or lower status than others with whom I share a scene? Does my status change in the play?*

Race, Culture, and Nationality

A playwright may choose to write about people of a specific race, culture, or nationality. While there are many traits that make characters unique from one another there are also traits that make characters similar within a culture or nationality. When you encounter this in a play, it is necessary to acknowledge the influence this has on your character. The cultural narrative informs the ways in which the characters interact. In *Race* by David Mamet, it is crucial that you understand the racial narrative from which the characters see the world, as the play is in large part dependent on it. In *A Raisin in the Sun* by Lorraine Hansberry, Asagai reminds Beneatha (Bennie) about what she said to him when they first met:

. . . You came up to me and you said . . . "Mr. Asagai—I want very much to talk with you. About Africa. You see, Mr. Asagai, I am looking for my identity!" [He laughs.] (Raisin in the Sun 1.2)

These lines take on greater poignancy if heard from the point of view of Bennie's racial narrative: that of a young American black woman who has been reared to hold her head high, but feels out of touch with her African ancestry. Though she has pride in her heritage, she lives in a place and time when by and large it is the white culture that determines the standards of "success": from the location of the "best" neighborhood to the most desirable texture and style for hair.

Ask yourself: *Has the playwright indicated my race, culture, or nationality? If so, what specifically is it? How does it influence who I am? How does it manifest in my behavior?*

Spirituality

For some characters and plays, spirituality has great significance. Many individuals believe and trust in a spiritual force or a power greater than themselves (this includes powerful individuals and governmental structures), sometimes without realizing it. Identifying where you lay your personal trust or fear may help you connect with the character's beliefs. Whether or not you (the actor) believe in the spiritual forces in a play is irrelevant. If you have committed to a role in which spirituality is significant, you must take into account the spiritual aspects of the *Who am I?* and the play as a whole. Joan La Pucelle (Joan of Arc) in *Henry VI Part 1* is an highly spiritual character. Below, she calls on spirits to help her to defeat the British in battle:

Now help, ye charming spells and pariapts,
And ye choice spirits that admonish me,
And give me signs of future accidents (Henry VI, Part 1 5.3).

Spirituality can be difficult to interpret. It requires first imagining a source of power outside of yourself, whether it be God, the devil, an angel, or some other figure, then determining how that source influences and affects you, and finally allowing it to do so. However, if you find that spirituality is not significant in a particular play, you need not address it.

Ask yourself: *Do I have a sense of spirituality? Is it from organized religion? If so, which one? Do I feel that life is predetermined? Do I believe goodness is rewarded and evil punished? Are spiritual beings or elements referred to in the play? How do these forces affect me?*

Vulnerability

In a well-crafted play, every word a character says will have been written with specific meaning. Identifying what the character sees and hears goes a long way to answering *Who am I?*. In life, hearing someone say, "It is raining" will have different meanings depending on the listener. For someone about to go on a picnic, the words spell disaster, while for an actor who must be inside for a long technical rehearsal, the words may not mean much. In life, we listen and see the world through the lens of our needs and concerns in the moment.

Ask yourself: *How do I, as the* Who am I? *hear what the other character said? What does it mean to me, as the* Who am I?.

Discovery

It is important to take in the world through the senses of the character as defined in the text. Guard against being alert and aware only when you have lines and "tuning out" when you are not speaking. A character in a scene may not have any lines, but the playwright has put that character on stage for a reason. Pay special attention during these times. What is being said that you, as the *Who am I?*, are meant to hear? You must see as the character sees, listen as the character listens, and feel as the character feels.

While the rehearsal process is a great opportunity for you to make important discoveries about the character, it does not end there. Often you can make interesting and important discoveries about the character in the performance run. Sometimes the fact that you are being observed by an audience can shed light on aspects of the *Who am I?* that you did not see in rehearsals and early readings. It may happen in live performance that an audience will respond to some event, action, or expression in a way that was not anticipated in rehearsal. This response might lead you to see that moment, and perhaps the entire *Who am I?*, in a new and meaningful way. Perhaps you notice that the audience laughs at an incident that never seemed funny in readings and rehearsals or, conversely, the laugh you expect fails to come. Take note of these natural audience responses and work with them, but don't fall into the trap of deliberately overacting anticipated moments, as this will disrupt yourself from living truthfully in the moment.

QUESTIONS AND ANSWERS

1. **Question:** What does it mean to "hear as the character hears?"
   Answer: We normally do more than listen passively when words are spoken to us. The words, phrases, and sentences trigger meaning in us. We interpret what is said based on several factors. What is our mood? What is our background (if any) with this person? Is there some prior experience we are bringing to the interaction? For example, in *The Zoo Story* Peter can interpret Jerry's statement "It's a nice day" as "Oh, no, this guy is going to ask me for money" whereas, someone else might ask himself, "Is this person crazy?" and a third listener might be glad of the chance to connect with a stranger.

2. **Question:** How do you know what might be an appropriate way to hear a given line?
   Answer: The way in which a line is interpreted depends on what the listener is concerned about at the time the utterance is made. The line "It's a nice day" triggers a reaction in Peter. For Peter, enjoying the privacy of his Sunday afternoon in the park is paramount. Jerry shows up as an intrusion and, if you are playing Peter, you might consider this. Further, your polite response, as Peter, to Jerry, can conceal rather than reveal your disappointment that someone has invaded your space.

3. **Question:** Are there other ways that the line can be heard by Peter?
   Answer: While there are other ways that Peter may hear the line that Jerry utters, the point is to always open up an inquiry in your work on a role, by asking the question *How do I,* as the *Who am I?,* hear the line that the other character says? Hear with the ears of your character. There can be a very big difference between the way you, the actor, hear a given line and the way that your character hears it. This helps you to consider possible ways that the line is heard, which will lead you to ask more questions in order to begin to answer the first question, such as *What is my character concerned with at this time that may inform the way he listens?*

4. **Question:** Does this mean that listening is more important than speaking?
   Answer: Listening and speaking should be given equal importance. It is interesting that sometimes actors put enormous emphasis on

rehearsing their lines that they say and how they should say them, but not on the lines they hear and how they should listen to them.

5. **Question:** Do all roles require some trasformation in order to avoid just "being yourself"?

Answer: Transformation implies change. In essence you are changing yourself in playing a role. Sometimes, there is very little change required. A character may be very close to you in body, dialect, ways of seeing the world and similar needs and patterns of expressing the self. Sometimes it is enough for you to use yourself, as you are, with little or no adjustment. However, you must still commit to specific objectives, actions and the ways in which the actions are played to help make the character distinct from yourself.

CHAPTER

Where am I? and When am I there?

IN A WELL-WRITTEN PLAY, THE CHARACTERS HAVE DISTINCT ways of viewing the world, informed by the places and times in which they live. You must use your imagination to explore place and time in all of their details, as observed through the senses, mind, and emotional life of the *Who am I?*. Imagine yourself as a person born and brought up in present-day New York City. A stranger approaches to ask a question. What is likely to run through your head? Now imagine visiting your country cousin in a small Texas town. A stranger approaches you there. Would you view the person differently and react differently? Picture the country cousin in her little town, where no one is a stranger, but imagine the year is 1929. Your cousin is an unmarried woman of 24. The town spinster? "Over the hill" and hoping to marry any man who will have her? Picture that woman, age 24, in New York City today. Picture New York City in 1929, just after the crash of the stock market; imagine desperate men who feel like failures as they watch their riches crumble away. If a scene is set in present-day Chicago, then you may already have background knowledge of that place and time. If a scene is set in seventeenth-century Paris, learn about that time and imagine as much of the particular environment as possible. In all these cases, *Where am I?* and *When am I there?* profoundly influence the actions of every character.

Designers

Theatre artists, such as set, lighting, and sound designers, contribute greatly to creating a sense of place and time. This can be done realistically, with items such as antique furniture and other elements from a specific period, and suggestively with light that creates tree shadows and the sounds of chirping crickets or passing traffic noise in a city setting. Your work as actor is to determine what these sources mean to you and allow yourself to be vulnerable to them. It is not a designer's job to make the surrounding world resonate in you. While a set designer can create a splendid forest-like environment as the setting for a production of *A Midsummer Night's Dream*, it is up to you as, for example, Hermia, to immerse yourself into the experience of being in the woods at night. That includes hearing the sound of an owl, seeing shadows pass, allowing yourself to be vulnerable to hidden dangers, and picturing what those dangers might be from Hermia's point of view, as you look for Lysander. Although you, the actor, know, that the actor playing Lysander is "off-left" waiting for his entrance, off-left does not exist for you, as Hermia, because in that direction Hermia sees woods that seem to go on and on like an endless maze. Somewhere in those woods is the love of your life. But where?

Imagine the given place in all of its details, as the character would experience it. If allowed, your imagination will take over, seeing and hearing details of a specific environment. Further, having "seen" and "heard" these details, continue to allow your imagination to define what these details mean. As Lyubov, in *The Cherry Orchard*, what significance might an old baby crib have for you? Allow your imagination to see your daughter Anya as a newborn baby, to feel her weight as you lay her in the crib for the first time—a crib that has been in the family for generations—and allow these elements to warm your heart. What might the vast and empty space with the lone tree mean to you, as Vladimir in *Waiting for Godot*? Allow your imagination to envision a vacant universe, and allow it to frighten you. What might your mother's bedchamber mean to you in the title role of *Hamlet*? Use your imagination to see your uncle, who murdered your father, sleeping beside your mother, and allow that to affect you.

Sources

These "things" that you see, hear, feel, taste, sense, and think—real or imagined—are called "sources" in this method. A source might be present (another character, a set piece, or a sound effect) or it might be in your imagination (an image of another character, a beautiful garden off stage, or the imagined sound of an unseen lover playing a classical guitar). There are times in a play when a character refers to sources that are not seen on stage. This may be due to a spare set design, a tight budget, or realistic restrictions of what can be constructed on a stage. Birch trees are symbolically meaningful and directly referred to in Act IV of *The Three Sisters*, as are the cherry trees throughout *The Cherry Orchard*, though it is unlikely they would be incorporated into set designs. The moon in *Romeo and Juliet* is almost important enough to be considered a third character in the famous balcony scene.

Form a clear and specific sense of those sources directly or indirectly referred to in a play. Some actors are particularly attuned to sounds, while others connect with touch, and others to the sight of things. Utilize your particular way to experience these sources. If you truly *experience* the sources through your senses, the audience will begin to experience them through their senses as well, thereby deepening the overall experience of the theatrical event. Through the actors and designers, the audience can become captivated by the imaginary world of the play and begin to enter into the given circumstances through its own imagination. In *To the Actor*, Michael Chekhov explains this is how a loop is created that connects actor with audience:

> *The actors who possess or who have newly acquired a love and understanding for atmosphere in a performance know only too well what a strong bond it creates between them and the spectator. Being enveloped by it, too, the spectator himself begins to "act" along with the actors. A compelling performance arises out of a reciprocal action between the actor and the spectator. If the actors, director, author, set designer and, often, the musicians have truly created the atmosphere of performance, the spectator will not be able to remain aloof from it, but will respond with inspiring waves of love and confidence (Chekhov 1953, 48).*

However, be on guard to keep your focus within the multidimensional imaginary world of the *Who am I?*. Shifting your focus in order to assess or appreciate audience response will weaken the cycle to which Chekhov refers.

Having a clear sense of *Where am I?* as you play a character will also help the audience to more fully experience a specific environment and its atmosphere beyond what may be present in the set, lights, sound, and costumes. If you, as the character, see cherry trees off-right, you help engage the audience's imagination to see them, as well. You, as Varya, might personalize what the cherry trees mean to you, giving the moment of sensing them greater richness if you are vulnerable to that meaning. As Varya, you might consider that the fate of the cherry orchard could mirror your own fate, which lies in the balance, as the house may be sold to pay the mortgage and, therefore, your home and, consequently, your status, would change. As Varya, you might visualize the cherry orchard without its trees, generating a melancholy feeling. You must find a way to make places, things, people, and desires meaningful so that you are vulnerable in dealing with them. Melancholy, joy, or passion are not generated out of just *saying* the lines, but also through finding ways to "personalize" sources around you referred to *by* the lines, whether those sources are real, such as a piece of furniture, or imagined, such as a row of cherry trees. Defining and fully imagining the atmosphere of a specific locale can also help you, as the *Who am I?*, enter into the imaginary circumstances of a scene and evoke within you an attitude or emotion appropriate to the specific situation.

In this approach there should always be a source (or sources) that feels alive for you. The term "where I'm at" is apt here. It means that you are always focused on someone or something, wherever you are physically on the set and within the lines of the script. It can be a wet piece of wood that you attempt to dry for a fire or an image of your beloved. If it is of a beloved, then imagining more than a picture, but a living, breathing entity is crucial. For you, as Tuzenbach in *The Three Sisters*, a source can be Irina and your own thoughts in the form of a mental "pep talk" about how to win her. As Hedda Gabler, the source can be you, as you pace up and down, focused on an image of yourself 12 inches in front of your face having made an important decision that might have serious negative consequences. That image of you can change fluidly into another image of what the negative consequences would be, and so on. Sources can be the scent of a rose, the sound of a bird chirping, the feel of freezing winds around you. It can be a mental narrative of how women are supposed to behave, if you are playing Torvald, and a sudden realization that you have no sense of yourself as a human being, if you are playing Nora in *A Doll House*.

Many of these sources are a necessary product of your imagination. You must define these sources, imagine them, and allow yourself to be affected by them, as they become part of your environment internally and externally. Creating sources should come from your imagination and the play itself. The written word is your partner in creating the world of the given circumstances. Ideally, you should have done so much of this work at home and in rehearsal that everything is accessible and alive for you in performance, setting you free to focus on pursuing *What do I want?* (which is examined in detail in Chapter 3).

The Play as a Guide to Establishing *Where am I?*

The question *Where am I?* doesn't end with defining the imaginary places in which the events in a play occur. The question also means exploring and defining what those places mean to you, as the *Who am I?*, and how you feel about those places.

The setting of each scene has been chosen by a playwright because it is meaningful. Sometimes playwrights will provide abundant information through an introduction or through dialogue. In some plays, the location must be discerned through the language of the play, while in others there is no clear description or indication of the locale through the language. August Strindberg describes the setting in lengthy and specific detail before the dialogue begins in *The Ghost Sonata*:

> *The first two floors of a facade of a new house on a city square. Only the corner of the house is visible, the ground floor terminating in a round room, the second floor in a balcony with a flagpole. When the curtains are drawn and the windows opened in the round room, one can see a white marble statue of a young woman surrounded by palms and bathed in sunlight. On the windowsill farthest to the left are pots of hyacinths—blue, white, pink* (The Ghost Sonata *stage direction*).

He continues on with his description for another seven paragraphs. Conversely, Samuel Beckett is sparse in describing the setting in *Waiting for Godot* as "A country road. A tree." He is more forthcoming in describing the setting in *Endgame*:

> *Bare interior. Grey light. Left and right back, high up, two small windows, curtains drawn. Front right, a door. Hanging near door, its face to wall, a picture. Front left, touching each other, covered with an old sheet, two ashbins. Center, in an armchair on castors, covered with an old sheet, Hamm. Motionless by the door, his eyes fixed on Hamm, Clov. Very red face. Brief tableau* (Endgame *stage direction*).

Folio editions of William Shakespeare's plays sometimes include a brief statement about where a scene is taking place and sometimes they do not. In the opening scene of *The Tempest*, *The Riverside Shakespeare* offers: "The Scene: [A ship at sea;] an uninhabited island." For *A Midsummer Night's Dream*, it is only through the dialogue that the reader can determine that the opening scene takes place in Theseus's court. When few details are specifically provided, use close readings of the play and the unlimited qualities of your imagination to begin to determine the *Where am I?*.

Although determining general locations can be a simple task, defining and refining details about the place and what they mean to the *Who am I?* can be challenging. Give yourself plenty of time to use your imagination in exploring location and what it means to you as the character. For one play, this can mean seeing yourself in a mirror that hangs on a wall downstage in front of the audience, although the set does not actually include a wall and mirror. It can mean "hearing" rain come down as you look out of an imaginary window, determining what the rain means to you, as the *Who am I?*, and allowing yourself to be affected by it. If you, as the *Who am I?*, see, hear, feel, smell, taste, in short, *immerse* yourself in important elements of the imaginary world around you, then the audience, too, will begin to experience them and, therefore, the essence of the play. However, all of this work must be done beforehand in rehearsal and private work alone, so that it is alive for you in performance.

Owing to the impossibility of building a replica of the historic battlefield in which the event in the play occurs, Shakespeare asks his audience to imagine some of those elements of that place through the Chorus speech in the prologue to *Henry V*:

Suppose within the girdle of these walls
Are now confined two mighty monarchies,
Whose high upreared and abutting fronts
The perilous narrow ocean parts asunder:
Piece out our imperfections with your thoughts;
Into a thousand parts divide on man,
And make imaginary puissance;
Think when we talk of horses, that you see them
Printing their proud hoofs i' the receiving earth;
For 'tis your thoughts that now must deck our kings,
Carry them here and there; jumping o'er times—(Henry V prologue).

While the actors can help create a sense of place, Shakespeare knew that it takes an active imagination on the part of the audience to appreciate the event. However, playwrights do not normally include dialogue asking the audience to help out. They assume, if the actors do their job, the audience *will* imagine. Addressing the question *Where am I?* in order to define the place and what it means to the *Who am I?* is a vital part of your job as an actor. An audience comes to a play knowing that the events are not real. Most audiences do expect a bit of help, via props, costumes, and set pieces in injecting themselves into the world of the play. The audience's imagination is helped greatly through the actor living truthfully within the imaginary environment conjured up by the playwright. It is crucial, then, that you use *your* imagination as the primary means for entering into the fictional environment of the play. To the extent you are able to do this, so, too, will your audience.

What *Where am I?* Means to You, as the Character

Location affects both who a character is and his behavior. In the most direct situations, the playwright will hint or reveal through the dialogue what this place means to this character. As you work, be specific about the place and the character's relationship to it. In Anton Chekhov's *The Cherry Orchard*, while Varya is the adopted daughter of Lyubov, the owner of the cherry orchard, she is also the mistress of the house. This is evidenced by her possession of the keys until she hurls them to the floor after the estate is sold to Lopahin. In the time and place that Chekhov wrote, to be the keeper of the keys to an estate meant an elevation of status in the person who kept them. Chekhov's dialogue reveals Varya's changed relationship to the *Where am I?* through Lopahin's line, "She threw these down [the keys] because she wanted to show that she's not the mistress here anymore" (*The Cherry Orchard* 3). "Here" is referring to the cherry orchard estate. In playing Varya, your exploration of the question *Where am I?* includes taking into account Varya's status, which you may have already defined through addressing the question *Who am I?*. As Varya, how you move through the house, how you conduct your physical activities, and how you interact with servants should be informed by where you are and your relationship to and status in that place.

Consider the significance of the park bench that Peter visits every Sunday afternoon to escape his family life in *The Zoo Story*. This place has special meaning to the *Who am I?*, which requires, you, as Peter, to make it especially important by personalizing it. Imagine the environment of which the bench is a part. Imagine the solitude; the sense of peace and serenity that comes from your Sunday afternoon visits to this bench with your book, your pipe, and all the rest of what makes this place special to you. The experience of Jerry entering "my place" and disrupting "my privacy" is all the more immediate if you take ownership of the environment through your imagination and senses. Imagine and experience the climate that Jerry describes as "sun-drenched." Personalizing it also means that the way in which you imagine the place may be somewhat different from the way another actor, as Peter, might imagine the place. You might be more inclined toward and responsive to a feeling of the place, while another actor might be more inclined toward and responsive to a visualizing or a combination of hearing and visualizing of the place. Both can be equally effective, though they are different. You have freedom to explore the *Where am I?* with *your* senses and *your* imagination, which are just as valid as any other actor's.

After imagining this place all around you, allow yourself to simply be affected by it. Is it somewhat secluded? What do you see when you look left, right, behind, and straight ahead? Feel the warmth of the sun on your face. Imagine hearing the blare of a taxi's horn outside of the park and let it annoy you. Perhaps, because the bench is somewhat hard, you bring a pillow to sit on. Adjust it and get comfortable. Taste the tip of your pipe and smell the resin of tobacco. What book are you reading, what page are you on, and how interested are you in reading on? Know that Jerry's appearance disrupts your reading, so perhaps you are in the middle of an exciting paragraph. Allow his appearance in "your place" to annoy you.

Some Areas to Investigate

When you explore *Where am I?*, begin with a "big picture" location. Most plays are set in a single town or city, or a single locale, with individual scenes that take place in defined locations within that larger area. Begin with the overall setting, and then you can narrow it down to specifics, which will almost certainly change from scene to scene. Do not stop with a simple answer such as "In my apartment in a big city," but begin to create a narrative, such as: "I'm standing at the stove cooking dinner in the kitchen of my crummy walk-up flat in downtown Chicago on a miserable winter day." Then dig deeper to expand the narrative. You can probe further by continually asking yourself, "What is relevant and meaningful about my location at this moment?," and allowing answers to surface in you; answers that you then realize through your imagination. Continue the narrative, expressing what *Where am I?* and *When am I there?* mean to you, as the character: "I'm standing at the stove cooking dinner in the kitchen of my crummy walk-up flat in downtown Chicago on a miserable winter day" might now include "and if my spendthrift partner didn't have such expensive tastes, I would have more money to spend on myself" or "I can't wait until my beloved child gets home because I make all these sacrifices for him."

Offered here are examples of important areas and questions to ask in order to begin an inquiry. Each play will have its own specific areas for importance, so think of this not as a comprehensive list, but as a set of beginning guidelines, which you can adapt according to the needs of each role. It is hoped that the examples and questions provide you with a model, so that when you are cast in a play you will be sensitive to identifying areas of importance, asking questions that lead to specific answers, and making strong choices for *Where am I?* and *When am I there?*. Note that only simple suggestions are made for questioning a given area. It is trusted that you will take your work far beyond the examples provided.

Where am I? *in the World*

Plays can be broad in their focus or specific. It may be enough to know you are in the United States or Russia. Or on a spaceship called the *Enterprise*, hurtling towards undiscovered galaxies. Or in an unknown room in an unknown prison in an unknown, unfriendly country.

Ask yourself: *What am I told or what clues am I given as to the large setting of this play? Am I in a real place or in a more generic setting? Can I research the setting and if so, where? How does this place make me feel?*

Where am I? *in My Locale*

City slickers are different from country folk. A spy in unfriendly territory has different concerns than a soldier returning as a hero in his home town. Is the setting in a named city, such as New York? Does it have associations for your character or the audience?

Ask yourself: *Can I put a specific name to my locale? Does it exist in real life and can I therefore research it? Is this area friendly or unfriendly? Am I comfortable or feeling like an outsider? In what other way does the locale affect me?*

Where am I? *in My Immediate Space*

If you are in a scene that takes place in the bedroom of your *Who am I?*, you would have great familiarity with that room. Conversely, if you, as the *Who am I?* are visiting another character in their bedroom, your degree of familiarity or lack of familiarity with that room should be very distinct.

Ask yourself: *Am I indoors or outside? Is there a hot sun shining uncomfortably down? Am I in a specific building or room? Is the room large or small? What are the physical and sensory details of this particular area?*

What Does this Place Mean to Me, as the Who am I?

A kitchen can mean many things. Some of the happy associations might be comfort, warmth and family. In a different family it might be where people let their hair down and are willing to fight. One character may look forward to visiting a gravesite, while another may dread it.

Ask yourself: *Is it a place that makes me comfortable? Happy? Nervous? Sad? Why do I choose to be here? Am I called here or forced to be here by another character or by circumstance? Can I leave when I am ready?*

The Play As a Guide to Establishing *When am I There?*

The question *When am I there?* refers to the entire span of time encompassed in a play. It might be general, such as summer or winter. It might be specific, such as New Year's Eve, 1999. Time refers to the time of day as well. It includes not only the time that passes during acts, but also between acts. Static time is also meaningful within a play. Consider the park bench where Peter sits on a Sunday afternoon in *The Zoo Story* and contrast it with that same bench 12 hours or so earlier on Saturday at two in the morning. In the afternoon you can sit and meet a friend, enjoy the sights of people with lunch, parents with strollers, joggers, bicyclists, pigeons, and squirrels. In the wee hours, you might be on the lookout for muggers, drug dealers (either seeking them out, or avoiding them, depending on the *Who am I?*), and rats. Your sensitivity to the circumstances of that bench at different times enriches the dramatic experience for both character and audience.

Time is a context for understanding character and how character changes, because it relates directly to the given circumstances of a play. A first reading will yield general answers to the question, while more detailed answers require investigation. Some plays depict an actual historic event. There may be pictures, biographies, literature, movies, television shows, music, and sound recordings to analyze. Such resources can be useful in helping you to transform into the *Who am I?*. You can use authentic material, interview people, or listen to or watch recordings of real events, to lend authenticity and exact details to the *Who am I?*. In plays that do not depict actual historic events, you must use your imagination to fill in details. Consider Anya's train ride to Paris in *The Cherry Orchard*. Anya says, "I left just before Easter." Chekhov tells us in opening stage directions, "It is early May." How long was the trip? Three, four, five weeks? Look at a map of Russia and imagine the train routes, speeds and distances to cover in 1904. How many countries and borders needed to be crossed? How many languages would have been useful to know? What were the train stations like for Anya?

Real life events leave a healthy pile of raw material from which an actor can draw inspiration. While some plays may have associations with historic events, most references to time are limited to the "world" of the play. The fact that "some estate" goes up for auction on August 22 is meaningless outside the world depicted in *The Cherry Orchard,* but is crucially important to every character in the play. Even in those plays where time is ill-defined, such as in Beckett's *Waiting for Godot*, it is important to apply the principle, if only to recognize that time, a basic element important to human beings, is not clearly defined. It is logical to assume that most audiences might wonder just how much time has passed since Gogo and Didi began waiting for Godot. "Waiting" implies the passage of time; the implication that, like Gogo and Didi, we have all been waiting for Godot for a very long time, but he will likely never come.

If the playwright does not clearly delineate the passage of time, you may have to reconstruct a timeline, rather like a forensic investigator gathering clues. Is a birthday referred to? Is there a holiday or historic event to indicate a date? Has a candle burned down or a meal been eaten and cleared away? Did a week pass between the on-stage relationship and death of the partner? Or a year? Or 10 years?

David Magarshack, in his book *Chekhov the Dramatist*, carefully analyzed the events in the play and dates associated with those events in *The Three Sisters*. He used events revealed in and through the dialogue to construct an accurate timeline that helps address the question *When am I there?*. He concluded that the whole play covered events over a period of about three and a half years, as the play opens on Irina's twentieth birthday and concludes in the autumn of her twenty-fourth year. Act II takes place nine months after Act I, in February. The fire in Act III occurs a few months after the end of Act II. Therefore, over two years must have passed between Act III and Act IV (Magarshack 1960, 259-60). You can apply this same type of analysis to any play.

It is important to observe that most scenes have a beginning, middle, and end. You can think of this in terms of the "arc" of the scene. Most often for the *Who am I?*, the scene starts one way and ends another way with some sort of change taking place for the characters in it. It is useful to think of the arc of a scene in terms of its overall *shape*. Knowing the shape of a scene will provide you with a structure for your work.

What *When am I There?* Means to You, as the *Who am I?*

Use time as a context for imagining what changes might logically be happening in a play. Do not ignore the passage of time within a play, as it can lead to ignoring the changes the *Who am I?* might undergo from scene to scene. You may flip a page of the script and see that the next act opens "Five years later." Explore what those "five years" have meant to you, as the character. Allow time to affect your *Who am I?* within the pace of the play, which can differ from the pace of "real life" and require you to occasionally ignore the fact that such a change may not occur that quickly in the real world. As you ask yourself *When am I there?*, begin to observe that scenes begin one way and end in another way *in time*. This will help you to determine what a given scene is about and how the character changes within it.

Preceding Time

It is important to be specific in recognizing and defining what occurs in the time in which a given scene takes place, but also important to examine the events and changes during the time that preceded a scene. *When am I there?* includes events that happen off-stage during and between acts, as well. If you are playing Masha, consider the time that passes between acts of *The Three Sisters*. Your relationship with Vershinin, which begins in Act I as mild flirtation, is on the verge of an affair by Act II. Vershinin's desire for a sexual relationship affects the way in which you behave towards him in Act II. Indications of some changes that have taken place in the time between Act I and Act II are suggested in the dialogue. Vershinin, who makes long-winded speeches in Act I, no longer has much to say: "I'm thirsty. I'd like some tea." You, as Masha, have speeches that indirectly accuse Vershinin of treating you disrespectfully: "Rudeness upsets me, it hurts me, I actually suffer when I meet someone who lacks refinement and courtesy." You reveal your mistake in marrying Kulygin, implying that you prefer another man, (such as Vershinin), for a husband: "—I was married when I was eighteen. I was so afraid of my husband, because he was a teacher, and I had just finished school myself. He seemed terribly brilliant then, very learned and important. But now, unfortunately, it's quite different" (*The Three Sisters* 2).

Note that every sentence Masha speaks refers to time in some way, revealing how she has changed, and, thus, shedding light, indirectly, on who she was then, who she is now, and cluing you in, as Masha, to what she wants in the scene. The time in which Masha and Vershinin's relationship has been going on is important, because it affects the ways in which you behave toward one another. Further examination of the passage of time in the play reveals that over two years have passed between Acts III and IV, so their affair has been going on for a relatively long period by Act IV. This unseen passage of time means your love can deepen. As your love intensifies, the eventual break-up due to Vershinin's transfer is all the more painful to you. Chekhov does not tell you this information about the passage of time, but it can be reconstructed through an analysis of the play. By asking the question *When am I there?* you can assert that Masha has been in love with Vershinin for three-and-a-half years when he leaves her in Act IV. This fact can inform the way in which you play the final scene. It is clear in the text that Masha needs to be restrained when Vershinin says his final farewell to her. Immediately after leaving her she speaks in fragments: "My life's mixed up . . . I don't want anything now . . . I'll be quiet in a minute . . . It doesn't matter . . . What *is* the 'curving shore?' Why does it keep coming up into my head all the time? Why does it haunt me? My thoughts are all mixed up" (*The Three Sisters* 4).

In the imaginary time between scenes, change usually occurs, and you must be sensitive to it. For example, you, as the *Who am I?*, can exit angrily and determined to have it out with your mother-in-law (off-stage) only to enter later in the act having failed in your goal.

Does the dialogue suggest that you backed down? Does the dialogue indicate a feeling of embarrassment or shame? Did you really let her have it, and damage the relationship with your wife? Examine what the play indicates or suggests happens between acts and/or when your character is off-stage. Use your imagination to discover and define what happened and how it affects the character. Once discovered and defined, it will help you to prepare for your entrance with an appropriate emotional state of arousal and attitude.

Some Areas to Investigate

As with the question, *Where am I?*, it is important that you thoroughly examine the play as it relates to time. That means you must not only consider the time of day, but the year, if it is an important element. You must also consider how long you have been where you are. Sometimes, it is enough to simply know that a play is set "during the day." However, often it is important to define specifically *When am I there?*, which can include the year (think of the significance of September 11, 2001, versus "September" in an unnamed year) as well as the circumstances, such as one week after the death of your mother.

When am I There? *in a Large Time Frame*

Some playwrights specify a year or specific events (Christmas Day, the Cold War) that allow you to narrow the time frame of the play. Others may appear to be "present day" and have some fluidity as to just when they are set.

Ask yourself: *What am I told or what clues am I given as to the time this play takes place? If the play says "present day" how far is the actual "present day" from the time the play was written? Do I need to adjust for that and if so, how? Has the director chosen to alter the setting of the play, and how does that affect me?*

When am I There? *Within the Year*

Winter settings generally call for bundling up; summer settings may be more revealing, which means dealing with different costumes in your work. The cold can affect the *Who am I?* The holidays may put stress on your characters. Birthdays signal growing older. Weddings approach, anniversaries are celebrated. Grave sites are visited upon the anniversary of a death.

Ask yourself: *What is the specific date or day or month or season? Why is this time significant to me?*

When am I There? *Within the Span of 24 Hours*

Late nights may mean fatigue and your guard is down. Early mornings make some people grouchy. It's seven in the evening, and my loved one said she'd be home at five. Am I worried? Or maybe irritated because we are going to be late to an important engagement?

Ask yourself: *Is it a specific time of day or night? How does the daylight or darkness affect the scene?*

What Does this Time Mean to Me as the Who am I?

The same time or the same time of day might mean different things to different characters. A mother may eagerly anticipate the peace and quiet of her child's bedtime, while the child is doing everything possible to stay awake. It is important to address the question of what the time means to the *Who am I?*.

Ask yourself: *Am I celebrating a birthday that makes me feel "past my prime"? Am I thrilled to be turning Sweet Sixteen? Is today the day I must deliver bad news? Is tonight the night I will finally go on the date I have been anticipating? Am I a flower child in San Francisco just as the Age of Aquarius is dawning? Do I look at the future with excitement or just hope I can stick around long enough to earn the gold watch and retire from my job?*

Where am I? and When am I there? need to be addressed thoroughly in every role that you play. You could conclude that establishing *Where am I?* and *When am I There?* is a process that goes on forever. Yet every actor has a finite amount of time to invest in a role. These questions should frame an ongoing inquiry. Exercise care in exploring and answering them through disciplined analysis. Invest your time wisely in defining those particular sources that directly affect your character and serve the needs of the play. However, the analysis is weakened if it remains purely an intellectual exercise. Allow the words encountered during analysis to evoke images, sounds, feelings, and smells. Through these imagined elements your human instrument will connect you to *Where am I?* and *When am I there?*

It is the heart of transformation when you allow yourself to be sensitive to what you imagine. It requires allowing yourself to be vulnerable emotionally, physically, intellectually, and sometimes spiritually to the circumstances. Do not hold your breath, but breathe through the experience of imagining the place, as indicated in the play; breathe through the process of becoming the *Who am I?*. Give yourself time and leave yourself room for discovery. Allow for the possibility that once these questions are answered, they can deepen or shift from experiencing them through rehearsal and even in performance. An "aha" moment can be experienced by answering these questions and living within them in the scene. For example, in rehearsal for *The Three Sisters,* you as Tuzenbach, in the time just before you are killed in a duel, are alone with Irina in the backyard of the estate. Knowing you will likely be killed, you ask her to look out at the birch trees. You may discover in that moment that you're not just in the backyard but in "heaven" of a sort because your lover is totally accessible to you, even if only for a moment and—to answer "when"—is to respond with: It is the last, most important moment of my life because, if I reach out to her in the right way, she will always remember me, somewhere in time.

QUESTIONS AND ANSWERS

1. **Question:** Can you address the question of time independently of place or the question of place independently of time?
   Answer: *When am I there?* is informed by *Where am I?* and vice versa. The two are intimately related. For example, San Francisco was a very different environment than Dallas on August 12, 1969. While time is an international constant, aside from time zone differences, the way in which a given time is experienced, and its meaning, can differ vastly. Many people celebrated the end of World War II, but the experience of the ending differed from place to place, from small places (like one household to another, city to city, or country to country). The questions should be addressed together if at all possible.

2. **Question:** Does the *Where am I?* inform your dialect?
   Answer: Not always. Consider Tennessee Williams' play *Eccentricities of a Nightingale.* The play is set in a Mississippi town. All of the characters grew up in the area, although one character attended school in the northeast and one character is a traveling salesman. As an actor playing the role of Alma, addressing the question *Where am I?* should take into account *When am I there?,* which includes the time period as well as how long you have lived where you live. For Alma, a Mississippi dialect is appropriate to the play and it's your job as actor to adopt the dialect to the point whereby you embody it. What this means is that you should get so comfortable with speaking the dialect that you do not have to focus on "getting it right" which will distract you from living

truthfully under the imaginary circumstances of the play. While for you, Alma, a decidedly specific and clear Mississippi accent is in keeping within the play, for the salesman it is not necessarily so. The play does not indicate where the salesman is from. Therefore, you and/or the director can choose to make the salesman from Chicago, for example, visiting the town on business. This then would require you, as the salesman, to take on a Chicago accent and do so in the same way that the actor playing Alma does: by embodying it to the point whereby it is part of you. Keep in mind, too, that a dialect can change slightly depending on the experience the character is undergoing. For example, the rhythm and pace of the Mississippi dialect, while naturally slow, with a drawl, can become quick and choppy if the character is under emotional diress. A talented playwright, such as Williams, will hint at such things in the way that the dialogue unfolds.

3. **Question:** Should the question, *When am I there?* take into account the character's past, even if it is not referred to much in the play?
   Answer: In asking the question *When am I there?* you should include *How long have I been there?* It may be important to the *Who am I?* if he is the "new kid on the block" and working hard to establish himself among strangers. Or maybe the comfort of a long association has made your character grow set in her ways.

4. **Question:** How do you approach portraying a character from a culture that you are unfamiliar with but need to understand in order to perform the role?
   Answer: Start first with the play itself. Determine how much of the play is informed by the culture. Is the culture of enormous importance to the play? If it is not, then less work is needed. If it is, then you must begin to examine the specifics of such a culure. It is important to begin to look at the culture in terms of a narrative that the people from that culture share. One way to get to know someone is by observing what they do. Narratives are always expressed in doing. By observing what they do, you can begin to consider what the narrative is out of which their behavior arises.

What Do I Want?

THE NEXT QUESTION DEALS WITH YOU, AS THE *WHO AM I?*, asking, *What do I want?*. Hamlet wants to restore order to Denmark. Maggie wants a child with Brick. Desdemona wants Emelia to reassure her. Lopahin wants the cherry orchard. Hedda wants power, and Martha wants to settle things with George once and for all and on *her* terms. These are some examples where there is general agreement as to what a character wants. Things are not always so clear.

Super-Objective and Objective

The term "super-objective" will be used to designate what it is that you, as the *Who am I?*, want throughout the entire play. Once you have chosen your super-objective, you can choose objectives (smaller steps towards the super-objective) to each scene. An actor will formulate many objectives for a given role, but each should support the super-objective designated for that character.

The term "objective" will be used to designate what it is that you, as the *Who am I?*, want that will lead to your accomplishing the super-objective. Often, the objective is related to what you want another character to do. The more specific your objective the more refined, focused, and well-rounded your performance will be. Your specific objectives will not only inform your behavior and the way you speak your lines, but your vulnerability and the way you listen to lines spoken to you.

The playwright does not specify objectives, nor do characters usually articulate them in soliloquies, monologues, or dialogues, at least not in a clear statement of "This is what I want." Sometimes this might seem like a missing convenience, but think of it rather as a freedom in that you are allowed to create objectives on behalf of the *Who am I?*. Different actors will arrive at different analyses of the same scene and may make different choices for objectives. That is part of what makes theatre interesting and keeps audiences coming back to plays they have seen before. Even if an objective seems fairly obvious, it is your job to articulate it to yourself in a way that is playable. Once achieved, an objective brings about a change in someone or something. Therefore, in formulating an objective it is important that you articulate specifically what that change will be so that you, as the character, can recognize it when (and if) if comes about. It is up to you to analyze the text for patterns of behavior and language and work to uncover what your character wants within each scene and throughout the play as a whole. You, the actor, should understand that while the character does not create, discover, or articulate objectives, you, the actor, do so *on behalf* of the character.

Once chosen, objectives will help bring you, as the *Who am I?*, to a single unifying purpose in the performance of the role. Without declaring an objective and taking action toward its fulfillment for a given scene your performance can become vague and unfocused, leaving the play's meaning open to a myriad of interpretations, many of which the playwright may never have intended.

Action, Intention, and Motivation

The term "action" is sometimes used by theatre artists to designate what the character wants (the objective). However, in this method, action (examined in greater detail in Chapter 5) is distinct from the objective; action is the means toward accomplishing the objective. Using this approach, keep the meanings of objective (*What do I want?*) and action (*How do I get what I want?*) distinct from one another, yet codependent in your work. Without actions to achieve them, objectives are meaningless. Without objectives to give them purpose, actions, too, are meaningless.

Numerous approaches to acting theory derived from or influenced by Constantine Stanislavski make use of the objective. Some approaches use the term "intention" as a substitute for objective. The problem with intention is that the term differs in meaning from objective. There is a difference between intending to do something and taking action consistent with achieving it, even if you, as the *Who am I?*, fail in your attempt. Think of this example from *Uncle Vanya* by Anton Chekhov: Vanya steals a bottle of morphine to commit suicide, but never does. You might consider that Astrov and Sonya intervene and talk him out of it. But you might also consider that he wants to be talked out of it, which might be articulated as the objective, *to get them to prevent me from commiting suicide.*

Make a distinction between what a character intends to do and actually does. While there is importance in recognizing intention, in this approach objective is different in that the character *always* takes action consistent with realizing the objective, regardless of whether or not the objective is, in fact, successfully achieved; in other words, make choices that can somehow be fulfilled through action. "Objective" is the appropriate term, because, whether or not realized, the objective always requires action for its realization. As action is the means for achieving the objective, you cannot choose an objective that might have action "invisible" to your audience, such as you, as Lady Macbeth, "*trying* to get my husband to murder Duncan." A more direct and effective objective is simpler: "To get my husband to kill Duncan" because, in using the former objective, what action can you take that will show "trying"? If your *Who am I?* is out of work and wants to get employed, then a clearer objective than "trying to get a job" is "to get Mr. Smith to hire me in his auto repair shop," or "to get Mrs. Smith to agree to pay me to babysit her little boy." You either succeed with Mr. Smith or Mrs. Smith, or you do not. If you meet an obstacle, you either overcome it or are stopped by it. A useful tip for determining what a character wants in a given scene and, in so doing, defining your objective, is to examine closely what the character actually does do, even if he is unsuccessful.

The term "motivation" has also been used in the same way as the objective. However, it is different from an objective in that it implies a psychological justification; the reason *why* the character does what he does. In *The End of Acting* Richard Hornby draws a clear distinction between the two:

> It is important to distinguish objective from motive. Motivation is a word tossed about far too casually in the theatre. It differs crucially from objective in that it looks backward, not forward, and is likely to be hidden and psychological rather than conscious and clear. [In] plays written before the realistic era and in many modern anti-realistic plays as well, it is quite possible for characters to have no motives at all in any deep sense, and modern actors are wrong when

they try to invent some, like deciding that Iago is motivated by an unconscious homosexual passion for Othello. But whether characters have motives or not, they always have conscious objectives if the play is any good at all (Hornby 2000, 166).

Address the question *What do I want?* seeking those objectives that would forward the events of the play. For example, Hamlet is a prince, the son of a king, which, for the Elizabethans, means he is of high status. Knowing that, in playing Hamlet, you would read the play and might articulate your super-objective as *I wish to do my princely duty and restore natural order to Denmark.* Once it is certain to Hamlet that Claudius murdered his father, Hamlet sets out to avenge his father's death and, thus, begins to restore order to Denmark. To do so Hamlet devises a scheme through a play (within the play) whereby he might come to know whether or not Claudius is guilty: *I'll tent him to the quick. If he but blench, I know my course.* Creating clear and specific objectives out of lines such as those and taking actions consistent with realizing those objectives serves your super-objective and the play.

Classical Plays

Generally in the classical period (prior to 1850 or so) objectives are revealed textually—that is, in and through the language of the plays. It is generally agreed that in the plays of Shakespeare, Christopher Marlowe, and Ben Johnson for example, the characters, for the most part, often say what they mean both to the audience and each other. Richard III makes one of his objectives clear in the opening soliloquy in Shakespeare's play of the same name:

Plots have I laid, inductions dangerous,
By drunken prophecies, libels, and dreams,
To set my brother Clarence and the king
In deadly hate the one against the other.

But this does not mean that objectives are always revealed directly in the language. Even if an opening soliloquy spells out what the character wants, it is still your job as an actor to determine objectives in later scenes that may not be immediately apparent. The play as a whole must be considered. In this passage, Desdemona clearly wants Emelia to reveal her personal attitude toward female infidelity:

DESDEMONA: O, these men, these men!
   Dost thou in conscience think,—tell me, Emilia,—

> That there be women do abuse their husbands
> In such gross kind?
> EMILIA: There be some such, no question.
> DESDEMONA: Wouldst thou do such a deed for all the world?
> EMILIA: Why, would not you?
> DESDEMONA: No, by this heavenly light!
> EMILIA: Nor I neither by this heavenly light;
> I might do't as well I' the dark.
> DESDEMONA: Wouldst thou do such a deed for all the world?
> EMILIA: The world's a huge thing: it is a great price.
> For a small vice.
> DESDEMONA: In troth, I think thou wouldst not.
> EMILIA: In troth, I think I should; and undo't when I had done.

Though you, as Desdemona, might see a clear possibility for an objective, you may not as clearly see what Emilia wants. If playing Emilia, upon first examination of the scene you may decide you want *to get Desdemona to have an affair*. But you might also consider that you want *to get Desdemona to stand up to Othello's abuses*. As the text does not clearly indicate what Emilia wants, further examination of the scene and its place and time within the entire play is in order. You may discern through reading the play that Emelia's husband (Iago) abuses her. Perhaps he cheats on her, which, when questioned by Desdemona, is a source for Emilia's attitude disclosed in what she says. Though not always easy to articulate specifically and clearly, creating well-defined objectives that can be realized through action will focus you, as Emelia or any other character. It will also sharpen your listening to the other actor, as character, because, just as in life, we listen from the point of view of our concerns, and our concerns manifest as wants, needs, and desires that find expression through action.

Modern Plays

In modern plays, beginning around the middle of the nineteenth century, this textual revelation is not always in place, but often finds expression only indirectly and, therefore, must be brought to the surface. "Subtextual" meaning is a second layer of meaning, below the surface of the spoken words. A character may speak a sentence with a literal meaning, but, in the moment expressed, be using those words for meaning something else. The line, "it's a nice day," that Jerry utters to Peter in *The Zoo Story* is much more about getting Peter to engage in a conversation than it is offering an opinion about the weather. More subtle than Jerry's speech, Vershinin's long-winded speeches, such as the one about the ignorance of the masses in Act I of *The Three Sisters*, are camouflage for seducing Masha. At the end of that speech in Act I, Vershinin concludes and Masha responds:

VERSHININ: Why, in two or three hundred years life on this earth will be wonderfully beautiful. Man longs for a life like that, and if he doesn't have it right now, he must imagine it, wait for it, dream about it, prepare for it; he must know more and see more than his father and his grandfather did. [*Laughs.*] And you complain because you know a lot that's useless.

MASHA: [*Takes off her hat.*] I'm staying for lunch.

Subtextual meaning can be expressed physically, such as when Stanley takes off his shirt in front of Blanche in Tennessee Williams' *A Streetcar Named Desire*. It could be argued that Stanley is simply feeling overwhelmed by the heat. But as an actor in the role of Stanley, to argue that is to miss an opportunity to use the possibility of subtextual, nonverbal communication as a playground for pursuing objectives that are connected to the *Who am I?* and forward the action of the play in a nonlinguistic way. For example, the subtext might include that Stanley is making it clear to Blanche that this is his house and he will behave in any way that he pleases.

Be aware that you will find many examples in modern plays where there are textual references to what the character wants. Consider Nora in Act IV of Henrik Ibsen's *A Doll House,* who explains to Torvald that she has discovered that she does not know who she is and wants to find out; therefore, she must leave him. She does forthrightly state what she wants: *I must try and educate myself—you are not the man to help me in that. I must do that for myself. And that is why I am going to leave you now.* You, as Nora, can articulate to yourself as an objective, such as *to get Torvald to treat me with respect* or *to get Torvald to release me without a fight.*

Prior Knowledge

Regardless of whether the objective is textual or subtextual, keep at the forefront of your thoughts that while you know how the play ends the character does not. You must always act without telegraphing your awareness of the eventual outcomes of the play. If your knowledge of the trajectory of the play is included in your immediate awareness during performance, it will have a dampening effect on your character's efforts to achieve the objective. If you are playing Masha, you, as actor, know that Vershinin leaves you in Act IV, but you, as Masha, do not know this until you learn that Vershinin and his army battery are being transferred, which occurs sometime in Act IV. If you allow Masha this knowledge it can diffuse your passionate pursuit of achieving an objective, such as *to get Vershinin to leave his wife for me*. Skillfully maintaining this ignorance about the future is often acknowledged by the expression *"the ability to live truthfully within the imaginary circumstances of the play."* Stanislavski used the term *as if* as a tool in large part to help the actor to better imagine and live truthfully within the given circumstances. In general you must act *as if* you do not know how things unfold, although, paradoxically, having read the play, you do know. You, as Masha, can choose to act *as if* you do not know that Vershinin leaves you at the end of the play.

Articulating the Super-Objective and the Objective

An actor will formulate many objectives for a given role, but each objective should lead toward an overall purpose: the super-objective that you have designated for that character. While there will be as many objectives as there are characters in a given scene, all of the objectives should serve the play. It is the director's job to make sure that the individual super-objectives and objectives are dovetailing into a coherent whole.

As Sonya in *Uncle Vanya*, you might choose to make your objective *to get Astrov to fall in love with me*, as evidence in the text strongly supports this choice. This objective would support a super-objective, such as *to have a sober Astrov as my husband, father of our three children, and provider for us all*. An objective, such as *to get Astrov to leave me alone*, would be inconsistent with that super-objective, as well as inconsistent with the entire play. Yet actors do sometimes make such choices at the peril of the play. Perhaps you personally do not find your scene partner attractive, although the play indicates a romantic attraction. Or you don't want to seem desperate. Or you would rather portray a brave man than a coward. If you accept a role in a play, you must commit yourself to the *Who am I?*, which might include being perceived as pitiful, disgusting, insincere, and shallow, all in service of the play as written.

Like viewing a tapestry, each of the character's objectives could be likened to threads in a pattern that contribute to the making of the whole. Suppose close readings of Natasha's role in *The Three Sisters* lead you to formulate her super-objective as *I want to acquire, protect, and hold sway over my family and homestead at all costs.* As the play is in large part about possession and dispossession, that super-objective strongly supports the overall meaning of the play and becomes a reason for you, in playing Natasha, to make specific choices for objectives that would help you to achieve that super-objective. These objectives form the pathway that leads you, as Natasha, to eventually take possession of the house from the three sisters. Suppose you, as Natasha, determine that your objective in Act I is *to get Andre to propose to me.* As Andre is the eldest sibling, he has control of the house, and the deed is in his name. By becoming his wife, you, as Natasha, will share ownership of the house with him, inheriting it altogether should he die. This objective serves you in *getting a home and family.* Consider that the play starts with friends and family in the house celebrating while Natasha is outside. However, the play ends with all of the sisters outside, dispossessed of the house and life as they knew it and Natasha inside, giving commands to servants and Andre alike. Natasha's super-objective represents a key element in the overall design of the tapestry image.

You might think in a "good" play, the characters each achieve their super-objectives. Sadly, for many characters, circumstances do not always end favorably. You might choose a super-objective that you know is not achieved, but might be crucial to the play's overall meaning. Consider Irina and Tuzenbach in *The Three Sisters*: After Irina spends the first three acts rebuffing Tuzenbach, by Act IV she begins to accept and even gets excited about a life with him. But she soon learns that he has just been killed in a duel and in the moment of learning the news she realizes that she loves him, although it is now too late. It should be irrelevant to you in a personal sense whether or not your character's objectives or super-objective are fulfilled. What should be most important is that your choice for the objectives and super-objective should be in service of the play's overall meaning.

Articulate the super-objective and objectives in positive and direct terms. For example, in the scene between Masha and Vershinin in Act II of *The Three Sisters*, the actor playing Masha could choose as her objective *to get Vershinin to stop aggressively pursuing me sexually.* However, this kind of choice is not as effective as a direct positive one such as *to get Vershinin to demonstrate respectful and romantic love for me,* which can help activate you, as Masha; giving you something specific to do that is both positive and direct. Also, while the super-objective might relate to attaining status, acquiring worldly goods, personal growth, or many other things, most often the objective should relate to something one character wants from another. Therefore, it should be articulated in those terms by actors when making choices on behalf of their characters.

When considering a super-objective for your *Who am I?* it can be helpful to think not only what it is your character wants throughout the play, but if the character's life were to extend beyond the play, what might the character want for that imaginary future time? This can help you begin to see those obstacles in the play that can be preventing the character from having what she or he wants overall.

Revealed Meaning

The objective sets up the context for the playing of actions. Objectives fully committed to through actions help reveal even the deepest of psychological interpretations of situations and circumstances. Regardless of the means whereby a character is analyzed and understood, the expression of character is dependent on the objective and the actions that would fulfill it. The objective can be based on psychological interpretations of character or information teased out and compiled from close reading of the play, especially one's intuitive sense of character. Plays, unlike novels, do not have details of circumstance and character clearly defined in a narrative. With the exception of stage directions, which may be scanty, plays are comprised mainly of dialogue. The actor fills in details that the playwright may only suggest within the dialogue.

After stating a clear super-objective for your character, you can begin to choose the objectives within each scene. You, as Lopahin in *The Cherry Orchard,* may choose to make your super-objective *to obtain legitimate ownership of the cherry orchard*, which is in keeping with the play. Your individual scenes could be defined through objectives, such as *to get Lyubov to acknowledge that I honestly tried to get her to pay the mortgage*. You, as Lopahin, can then say you did not practice deceit but legitimately purchased the cherry orchard. Clearly stated objectives help the actor find a way to reveal specific meaning even if that meaning seems ambiguous. The use of the objective sets you free to play action towards its accomplishment. Action helps to reveal the *Who am I?* by forwarding the events of the play. Action can help to generate conflict, as it is a means toward overcoming and surmounting obstacles encountered through interaction with other characters whose objectives may be diametrically opposed to your own. It can also help to generate harmony in helping to realize objectives with other characters that are more aligned to your own.

Stakes

The objective is always directly related to the needs of the character, articulated as what it is that you want. When playing a role, you, the actor, examine the text and decide what it is you want as the character and then set about taking action to fulfill that need. Needs imply importance. If you need something, then, logically, it is important to acquire it. It also implies there are consequences if the need is not fulfilled. You may sometimes play a character who has a deep need, but is not given to introspectively analyzing and expressing the need. You, as the actor, are charged with revealing that need even if your character is not openly "thinking" it. The term "stakes" is used to designate the consequences of fulfilling or not fulfilling the need. Stakes are an essential element to consider when articulating the objective you formulate on behalf of the character. For example, in *Cat on a Hot Tin Roof* you might determine that Maggie needs to have a child. Without one she is looked at as failing in her role as a woman and a wife. In *Hamlet* you might consider that Hamlet needs to avenge the murder of his father. Without avenging his death, order will not be restored to Denmark. In Martin McDonagh's *The Pillowman*, Ariel needs to get Katurian to confess. Without his confession and punishment, more children could meet the same fate as the others. Emotionally, physically, and intellectually committing yourself to an objective on behalf of the *Who am I?* includes recognizing what is at stake if the objective is not achieved. This means allowing yourself to be vulnerable to the possibility that things could end unfavorably for you, as the *Who am I?* although, paradoxically, you, the actor, know how things actually unfold.

Obstacles

Obstacles are those things that stand in the way of achieving your objective. If there were no obstacles there would be no conflict, and it is through conflict that drama is generated. As with stakes, it is imperative that you articulate the obstacles to fulfilling your objectives on behalf of the *Who am I?*. For Natasha, obstacles to achieving her super-objective of possessing the house include the fact that the sisters share the house with their brother, Andre. It is important that you recognize the obstacle implicit in your objective. Every well-formulated objective includes an obstacle to its fulfillment. Even the simple act of quenching one's thirst implies having to get up off the couch, get a clean glass from the cabinet, cross to the kitchen sink, fill it with water, and drink. Luckily for actors (and audiences), most plays are written about characters who want things that require overcoming meaningful obstacles. It is the struggle to overcome obstacles, not necessarily the ultimate success or failure, that creates great drama.

A Word About Listening

Sometimes actors will be criticized in their work for not listening to their fellow actors in a given scene or play. Or if they are listening, it is in a general way. The objective you choose should help create a specific listening. By fully committing yourself to the need of your character's objective, while maintaining the attitude of not knowing whether or not the objective is accomplished, you, as the character, would listen carefully, in an interested or filtering manner, to other actors as characters in a given scene. Often the expression of the accomplishment (or failed accomplishment) of the objective is revealed through communication in the dialogue. For example, in Act I of *The Pillowman* it can be strongly argued that Ariel wishes Katurian to confess to murder, although he is not the killer. Ariel can be listening for Katurian's confession through a phrase such as, "Yes, I killed the children." Although Katurian is innocent and, therefore, never confesses, it is entirely in keeping with Ariel that he should be listening to Katurian for a confession, as Ariel believes Katurian is the killer, and there is evidence to justify his belief. This active listening can help give you, as Ariel, purpose and focus during the scenes with Katurian, rather than simply running your next set of lines in your head or waiting for your cue to speak.

What Do I Do After I Get or Fail to Get What I Want?

What do I do after I get or fail to get what I want? can be answered in several ways. Sometimes the playwright answers the question for the actor by having the character exit. If the character stays in the scene after his objective has been accomplished, the actor, as the character, may choose to get more of what he wants, (*treat me more respectfully, if getting him to treat me respectfully* was the objective). Other times, you may make the choice to move on to another objective that serves the purpose of the super-objective. You may choose to have your character return to a prior unmet objective. For example, if you, as Nina, in Act II of *The Sea Gull*, accomplish the objective *to make Treplev go away*, you can then focus on a prior objective, before Treplev interfered, such as *to get Trigorin to fall in love with me*.

Always make your objectives primarily about those characters in those scenes with you. After Treplev's exit in Act II, he does not reappear until Act III. Treplev's next major scene is with his mother, as she fixes his bandage. It is indicated that sometime before the scene with Irina he was superficially wounded when he attempted suicide. You, as Treplev, should have created a new objective for this scene, abandoning the prior unfulfilled objective between Treplev and Nina. A new objective might be *to get my mother to intervene in the budding relationship between Trigorin and Nina*. This certainly serves as a strong choice for his super-objective, which might be articulated as *to share a loving relationship and a successful career in the theatre with Nina*. You, as Treplev, could make the suicide attempt a reaction to Nina's rejection, which might be articulated as an objective of *to get Nina to pay attention to me*. However, as Nina is not present in the scene, and Irina is beside you, bandaging your head, a stronger choice would be an objective that allows you to play action on the person present (the actor as Irina).

QUESTIONS AND ANSWERS

1. **Question:** Are objectives always about one character wanting another character to do something?
   Answer: Usually, but not always. There are many one-person shows in which the actor must use objectives indepedent of other actors. Even in a show with several characters, there may be points in which an objective is not about getting another character to do something. For example, in the very first few moments of *Waiting for Godot*, Estrogan is trying to take off his boot. His objective in those first few moments can be *to take off my boots*, which begins with one boot at a time. However, when Vladimir enters, his objective can change to: *to get Vladimir to help me get my boots off*.

2. **Question:** What if you share a scene with more than one character?
   Answer: You should have objectives for each of the characters in the scene with you that are in any way significant to your *Who am I?*. For example, if you are playing Masha in *The Sea Gull*, you share a scene

with Treplev and Medvendenko in Act I, so you will most be most effective with two distinct objectives. You can choose to get Treplev *to find me attractive* and to get Medvendenko *to continue to pursue me*. However, you can only focus on one action at a time, as it will defuse your energies to split focus. Therefore, you might play an action on Treplev, such as *to make him feel important*. This is consistent with your objective with Treplev. The objective with Medvendeko can be part of your focus, but not primary.

3. **Question:** What if you share a scene with a large ensemble?
   Answer: In a scene that includes many characters, it is impractical and perhaps impossible to define an objective for every character in the scene, particularly if the other characters are not significant to you, as the *Who am I?*. In such a scene, consider your super-objective and how those present can serve in obtaining it. This will clue you in as to whether or not the other characters are significant to your *Who am I?*. If they are significant then articulate that significance in terms of objectives. Even if you do not interact with them during the scene, articulating clear specific objectives for those characters will add depth and meaning to your *Who am I?*.

4. **Question:** Should you be thinking about the super-objective in all scenes?
   Answer: No. Once the super-objective is determined, then you should analyze the text for objectives that would serve the super-objective and lead to its accomplishment. The objective will contextualize a section of text. It will help define that section and make it distinct from other parts of the play. Your job as actor is to make that entire section about trying to accomplish that objective. This requires a short-term focus as you use the objective to create a mini-world that has a duration of that specific time. You, as the actor, should not get ahead of yourself and start playing the end of a scene in the middle of it. You need to focus and give yourself over entirely to accomplishing whatever objective you have for the time in which you have it. And you must do this night after night in rehearsal and performance. Actions, as defined, explained, and examined in the next chapter, will give you focus and purpose from moment to moment.

5. **Question:** How many objectives does a given role contain?
   Answer: Roles do not contain objectives. Objectives are created by each actor as he makes a role his own. Objectives are a means of defining what a particular section of a play is about. You can analyze a role in a play, such as Jerry in *The Zoo Story*, and understand that in the opening few moments Jerry appears and begins a conversation with Peter. However, you can take this further by creating an objective for the opening few lines, such as *to get Peter to engage in a friendly conversation with me*, which gives you, as Jerry, through the opening dialogue, a specific, uni-

fying and playable purpose. It helps you to make your acting succinct and about something specific that is consistent with the play.

6. **Question:** How do you know whether or not you have chosen the right objective?

   Answer: It's not productive to consider whether your objective is right or wrong. It is better to think of it as either serving or not serving both your super-objective and the play as a whole. Remember that your super-objective must serve the play. This requires you to understand what the play is about and what the playwright is saying. You can then begin to define a super-objective for the *Who am I?*. From the super-objective you begin to formulate objectives for the scenes in which you appear. These objectives should serve the super-objective. For example, you, as Richard III, might logically choose *to become king of England* as your super-objective. For you, as Richard in Act I, Scene II with Lady Anne, a strong objective is *to get her to agree to marry me*. You, as Richard, do not need to focus on becoming the king of England in the scene with Lady Anne. You need a *short term focus* of getting her to agree to marry you. This objective, if accomplished, helps you, as Richard, to achieve the throne.

7. **Question:** What if I'm in a play and rehearsals are beginning and, although I can see possibilities for objectives in certain scenes, I cannot articulate a super-objective that gives them a unifying purpose?

   Answer: Do without the super-objective initially and stay open to discovering what a strong and effective super-objective might be. Meanwhile, make strong, positive objective choices based on close readings of the play and see if they serve you in the role. If they do, stay open to discovering what those objectives have in common; what they suggest might be a super-objective that would unify them. It is certainly possible to play the role without ever discovering a strong and effective super-objective. However, you should still choose objectives for every moment on stage. Likely, those objectives will give you a strong indication of what your *Who am I?* wants overall.

How Do I Get What I Want?

Plays, AS WRITTEN, ARE TWO-DIMENSIONAL, BUT ACTORS (as well as directors and all those involved in bringing a play to life) need to approach plays as potential three-dimensional experiences, whose characters are revealed through action. In order to fit many events into a few hours or less, plays condense the experiences of life, giving an actor a short window of time in which to reveal an enormous amount of information about the character and the world of the play.

The ideas discussed in this chapter are not designed to replace learning lines, analyzing what a given scene is about, respecting the meter and alliteration in verse plays, and using your intuition and common sense. But to fully reveal a character, and transport the audience into the world of the play, it is important that every moment be fully realized through action. Directors, actors, and theatre educators often toss the word "action" around without defining it, assuming everyone knows what "action" is. Knowing how this approach defines and uses action will be crucial to moving forward in your work.

Some Common Definitions (And Why to Put Them Aside)

Sometimes "action" is used to designate physical movement, typically known as blocking. A director may say to an actor that her "action" is to "enter, look around the room, and then sit on the couch." While this meaning of "action" (to do something physically) matches the lay person's interpretation of the word, it is not how this approach defines it. Sometimes "action" is used to designate "activities." The director might block a play with activities such as a woman, returning home from a late night at her second job, taking off her rain coat, drying her wet hair with a towel, glaring at her couch-surfing husband, and pouring herself a drink. While activity is of enormous importance, it is not action as this approach defines it.

"Action" is sometimes understood as a verb used to designate interaction. One actor, as a character, might *convince* another actor, as a character, to come to terms with an abusive parent. "Action" in the verb approach is identified by verbs such as *to chastise, to please, to lecture,* and *to intimidate.* One can imagine the situation where a mother chastises a son for failing to call home while staying out past curfew. The mother chastises the son in order to fulfill her objective: *to get him to honor his curfew* or simply *to get him to come home on time.* However, the actor playing the mother, using the verb approach, *to chastise,* might produce the outward appearance of chastising through imitating or expressing what she, the actor, considers chastising someone to look like, without affecting the other actor, as a character, in an organic way.

Action Defined in this Approach

Action in this approach is the *act of committing yourself, as the Who am I?, to making another person, image, or object feel something.* In the example above of the mother and curfew-breaking son, try articulating the action in terms of how you, as the mother, attempt to make your scene partner, as the son, feel. If you can generate in your scene partner the experience of being chastised, it will be much stronger for him (and the audience) than just "acting like" or giving the appearance of chastising. You might try to make him feel *irresponsible* or *negligent* or *guilty.* By articulating action in this way you can see that the mother's focus in fulfilling the action is entirely on the son; committing herself to making him feel whatever she chooses. In this way you can avoid concerning yourself with trying to accurately depict what the behavior "chastising" looks like and focus directly on evoking a feeling in your scene partner.

Remember the prior example, where the overworked woman dries her hair and pours herself a drink? Here is one possibility for that scene, using this principle of action. As she enters, she sees her husband sitting on the couch. The actor playing the woman might choose as her objective *to get him to cut back on spending money.* The woman's action on the man upon entering might be *to make him feel guilty.*

The actor playing the husband might have as his objective: *to get her to quit her second job and pay more attention to me.* The man's action on the woman might be *to make her feel wrong.* Without dialogue, this opening section of the scene can be used for this silent communication between the two partners. Without this action, the scene is lost in focusing on activities, such as taking off a coat and pouring a drink. With action, the obligatory activities will still be fulfilled, but the scene is made potent, as the wife hangs up her coat while simultaneously playing the action *to make him feel guilty,* and he sits on the couch playing the action *to make her feel wrong.*

This approach to action differs from most in that it is wholly concerned with the actor, as a character, evoking feeling in another actor as a character, or in an image, or in a thing. You might choose to play the action towards the emotions (*to make someone feel sad, guilty, loved*). You might focus an action that appeals to the senses (*to make someone feel excited, safe, aroused*). You might play on psychological elements (*to make someone feel needed, rejected, pressured*). It is not necessary to put things in a particular category, but sometimes mentally searching within broad categories can help you lock in on the name for an authentic feeling to help you play action.

It may be helpful to think about this principle of action by comparing it with the way you accomplish results in life. You have probably noticed that people influence one another through emotional as well as intellectual means. Think of a recent political speech you heard or a pitch seeking a charitable contribution. How much were you affected by the intellectual arguments of the speaker and how much were you affected by the emotional connection the speaker made? If a newscaster told you "thousands of people were killed in recent flooding" you would probably shake your head and think "how awful." But would you be motivated to do something specific to help? Maybe make a donation, volunteer, or gather clothes and shoes and take them to a collection center? Take a moment now to use your imagination: picture seeing a friend (or even a stranger) standing outside his flooded home. Tears run down his cheeks. Everything he owns has been ruined. A moldy smell is in the air, the sound of thunder in the distance. More rain is on the way. For most of us, this emotional connection is what will motivate us to get involved.

It can be useful to think of your action in terms of "positive" or "negative." You might define your action as, for example, to make someone feel *special* (positive) or *unwanted* (negative). Consider a metaphor such as the "carrot" (positive) and the "stick" (negative) to get you started in making choices. Both a carrot and a stick can be used to achieve change—and you, as a skillful actor, will learn which action seems to best serve whatever scene you are currently playing.

Just as a skillful poet can evoke feelings in the reader of her poem, you as a character can use action to evoke feelings in another actor as a character and, in doing so, affect the audience, as well. Such feelings are at the heart of experiencing a play as it unfolds from moment to moment. The audience could sit at home and read the play, but it comes to the theatre to experience it.

This happens in subtle (and not so subtle) forms in advertising. For example, we are often motivated to purchase a product without a true need to have this product. An advertisement to buy a car might not suggest you check the odometer to see if your current car is getting old and needs to be replaced. Most advertisements will try to make you "feel" the thrill of the wind in your hair or the smoothness of the ride or the soft laughter of the beautiful girl sitting beside you or the security of your baby sleeping in his car seat.

The "How" of the Action

Once you are comfortable with this idea of action, you can further refine it using the "how" of an action. The how of an action is linked to the *Who am I?* of the character. In *The Three Sisters* an actor playing Olga might make an actor playing Natasha feel wrong, but in a gentle way, as gentility is part of who she is. A bully can choose to make another character feel fear in a *mocking* way. There are infinite ways to make someone feel loved, such as in a romantic way, in a sexy way, in a brotherly way, in a maternal way, in a spiritual way, or in a teasing way. You, as the *Who am I?*, can make someone feel stupid in a gentle way, in a brutal way, in a mocking way; you can make someone feel guilty in a dismissive way, in a caring way, or in a cold, cruel way. The how of the action, along with the action itself, is a prime vehicle for revealing the *Who am I?* of your character.

Bruce Katzman, a former teaching assistant and long-time associate of Gister, and teacher and practitioner of this methodology for many years, provides an excellent example of using the "how" of the action in a scene between Andre and Natasha in Act II of *The Three Sisters*: Natasha, in dealing with Andre in the opening scene of Act II, has the objective of wanting Andre to cancel a party, scheduled for later that night. She knows that Protopopov, her former lover, has arranged to take her for a sleigh ride that same evening and the party would interfere. At first glance, her text in the scene seems to be complaining and whining. But complaining and whining may not get her what she wants. What she wants is to preserve her marriage (after all, they are still newlyweds at eight months.). What she wants is for Andre to be compliant. What she wants is to get Andre to carry out her wishes; so she may have better luck using a carrot on Andre, rather than a stick. In other words, loving actions may produce better results than bruising actions. She needs Andre on her side. Her first line is *"Andre, what are you doing?"*. Andre, is in his study, with the door shut. She wants to get him to come out of his cave voluntarily, so, for an action, she might make him feel loved and desired in a seductive way. If he comes out of the room (which he does), she may then have to "turn down the heat" and make him feel loved and needed in a protective way—after all, she doesn't want to have sex with him, but she will use the promise of sex to get what she wants. Her skill in manipulating Andre in this way reveals a fundamental dynamic in their relationship, and she alternates the how of the action to great effect. She wants to warm him up, but not get him too warm. If he cools in his response to her, she will use her seductive skills to warm him back up. When she tells him he has to reduce his diet and eat only yogurt, she can do so in a shrewish (a stick action) or loving (a carrot action) way.

Alternating actions, or varying the how of an action, can provide the actor with an infinite set of possibilities to speak to the character's nature or truth. Katzman continues with another example from *The Three Sisters*: Masha is powerfully attracted to Vershinin, a fact first revealed by Masha's decision in Act I to stay for Irina's birthday luncheon, even after she had put on her hat and coat and was ready to leave. After the introduction of Vershinin, an old family friend newly arrived from Moscow (who also happens to be handsome, charming, and bright), Masha takes off her hat and declares, "I think I'll stay for lunch." We know how she feels about this attractive newcomer by what she does. Later, in Act II, Masha struggles with her desire to consummate a physical affair with Vershinin and her desire to not commit adultery with him.

Her actions alternate between making Vershinin feel loved and making him feel rejected. In those moments when she wants him to feel loved, she moves towards him. Her gestures, voice, and body language all are meant to make him feel wanted and loved. But when it gets too "dangerous," when her desire begins to get out of control, and she becomes fearful of adultery, her action changes—she begins to make him feel guilty, unwanted, rejected; she moves away from him, distances herself, won't look at him, until the rejection of him becomes too painful, the thought of losing him becomes too painful, the look of pain and despair in his eyes becomes too painful, and then she reverses her actions again, telling him once again through her movement, gestures, and voice that she wants him, loves him, and can't live without him. The repetition of this pattern—now I'm moving toward him, now away; now making him feel loved, now making him feel rejected—reveals to the audience that Masha cannot make up her mind; that she is indecisive, that she is conflicted, that she is torn. For you, as Masha, it is not possible to play two actions at the same time, but it is possible to play alternating actions in rapid succession. Two opposite actions will cancel each other out, but in rapid succession, an inner life may be revealed.

Using Actions with Images and Objects

Action can occur not only from one person to another person, but from a person to images and objects as well. If you fully commit to making a picture of a rival feel unattractive, you may start to feel an emotion as well. Human emotions do not always honor the boundary between reality and fantasy. Can you think of a time when seeing a violent image made you feel sick? When seeing a beloved pet's photograph calmed you down? When imagining the image of a confrontation with your boss made you nervous, even though the confrontation never happened? Seeing her wedding dress may bring a young widow to tears. Using images or objects demands that you focus clear and specific actions on a named target. Playing action on images can help students and beginning actors to reveal their characters more fully and short circuits a habit of too much internalizing or self-consciousness. When Julia observes the picture of her rival in William Shakespeare's *Two Gentlemen of Verona*, she might choose to "make her feel unattractive," and in the playing of that she may begin to feel "confidence" in proceeding with the objective of besting her rival.

Consequences of Playing an Action

This principle of action reaches beyond scene partners and sources and into the audience. Audiences attend plays to be a part of an entire theatrical event, from the dimming of the lights to the applause at the end. If it were otherwise, people would be satisfied with reading plays at home in the comfort of their easy chairs. But when you perform in front of an audience, the act of making someone or something feel on stage resonates. If, while on stage, you make another actor, as a character, *feel sad*, not only will the emotion surface in the actor, but it can surface in members of the audience, too. When members of the audience begin to experience the emotional current of the play, their reactions will affect the actors. In this way, an emotional loop is generated that travels from actor to audience and back. When this emotional looping is strongly felt, a play has "chemistry."

In plays where the aesthetic of the writing or the directorial approach calls for you as the character to speak to the audience, action can help you to generate a more direct experience. For example, at the very start of the famous balcony scene in Romeo and Juliet, Romeo has the line: "He jests at scars that never felt a wound," "He" referring to Benvolio, who makes fun of him for being in love. If the directorial approach to the play includes direct address, this line could be said to the audience with an action, such as to make the audience feel sympathetic. Further refined, this method strongly suggests that when you are called upon to speak to an audience that you focus on one audience member at a time, and play an action on that audience member, such as "feel sympathetic" or "feel sympathy for me." Making one member feel sympathetic will resonate in the whole, thus creating an experience that might otherwise have been missed had you only spoken the line to yourself.

Action is Anchored in the Objective

Before choosing your action for a scene, first you must determine your objective. Once you have determined the objective, choose the action that you, as the *Who am I?*, will do to fulfill this objective. The pursuit of the objective through actions moves the play forward. Characters want things, and then they grapple with obstacles, which creates conflict, keeping the play vital and alive. An actor might have several actions in the course of pursuing a given objective. You, as a character, might shift from one action to another action, if the first action has not led to the accomplishment of the objective. For example, with the objective *to get my son to agree to be more responsible by respecting curfew,* you might start by making your son feel *wrong.* However, several lines later you may change the action to making him feel *loved,* depending on what happens as revealed through the dialogue. If the scene is longer, and the son quite resistant to complying with your wishes, you might add making your son feel *guilty*, then *irresponsible*, then *pressured*, then *scared*. Such a journey is compelling to watch. Importantly, through the on-stage actions of making someone feel *wrong/loved/guilty/irresponsible/pressured/scared*, these feelings will resonate in the audience as well, generating a more intense moment to moment experience of the play.

If a person commits to playing an action, whether in acting or in life, then the person's own emotional life can come right along in its playing out. You will find that the act of fully attempting to make someone or something feel an emotion can trigger an emotion in yourself as well. If you, as Romeo, attempt to make Juliet feel desired, this can bring about a feeling of desire both in the actor playing Juliet and yourself, as Romeo. Conversely, if you, as a character, attempt to make your scene partner feel intimidated, it could lead to feelings of power in yourself (as the one playing the action) while it might lead your scene partner (as the one the action is played upon) to feel belittled or fearful. These played actions can lead to enhanced feelings when objectives are compatible between actors as characters, such as when a romantically involved couple both long for a deeper commitment, and only the terms of the commitment might vary and be the source of tension, or, as in the circumstances of *Romeo and Juliet*, outside sources are the real obstacles to the couple's future. Playing actions can lead to contrasting feelings between actors as characters when characters have entirely different objectives.

Action in Classical and Modern Plays

Most of the time in classical plays the approach to action is textual. This means that the language itself suggests action you might play in order to achieve your objective. Paulina in William Shakespeare's *The Winter's Tale* asks Leontes: "What studied torments, tyrant, hast thou for me?" Paulina calls Leontes a tyrant. If you are playing Paulina, choosing to make Leontes *feel bad* in some way, such as *disgusting* or *loathsome* rather than just naming him a "tyrant," can be a powerful choice that affects the actor as Leontes. Later, you, as Paulina, can play another action, such as to make him feel shame or fear, with:

When I have said, cry 'woe!' the queen, the queen,
The sweet'st, dear'st creature's dead, and vengeance for't
Not dropp'd down yet.

Be vigilant about not substituting action choices at the expense of other approaches to classic language, especially verse, such as defining antithesis, respecting the iambic pentameter, or breaking a speech down into specific thoughts, which, in addition to action, should be included in your work. This playing of action is a way of using the language to affect one another in order to accomplish the objective.

In modern plays the approach to action can be subtextual. This means that a given line may not necessarily reveal what is going on between the two characters. The actor must understand what is happening subtextually and out of that understanding choose objectives on behalf of the character and then set about playing actions to fulfill those objectives. When Sonya in *Uncle Vanya* asks Yelena: "Would you like your husband to be young?" that question is not as straightforward as it first appears. Through reading the play, one can deduce that what she really wants to know (the subtext) is this: Is Yelena romantically interested in Dr. Astrov, with whom Sonya is in love? Knowing this, you, as Sonya, can play subtextual action. You might choose to make the actor, as Yelena, *feel pressured* into revealing her true intentions, as she is married to Sonya's father, who is older. To refine the action even further, consider your action as Sonya is *to make Yelena feel she is being tested by a lie detector.* There are three questions in a row within the dialogue of the scene: 1) Tell me, truthfully, as a friend, are you happy? 2) Would you like your husband to be young?, and 3) Do you like the doctor? If Yelena answers them all "correctly" then you can have a friendship and you can trust Yelena and tell her all about your secret love. But if she answers incorrectly (because you, as Sonya, know the truth before you ask the questions), then you will withdraw back into your hidden and hostile shell.

Action, Objective, Paradox, and the Present Moment

The means to achieving a sense of truthfulness and believability in your acting resides in an important distinction: *While the actor knows the outcome of the play, the character does not.* You know that Romeo and Juliet do not live happily ever after, but through most of the play, the characters of Romeo and Juliet are not aware of this fact. There may be a few isolated instances (for example: Joan of Arc in William Shakespeare's *Henry VI, Part I*) where a character has knowledge of the future within the context of the play, but this should only happen when the playwright has written the character in that specific way.

It is not enough in and of itself to remember: "While the actor knows the outcome, the character does not." That is a place to begin in the formation of clear and specific objectives. The next step is to fully ground yourself in living believably within the imaginary circumstances of the play by playing action. By fully committing yourself on behalf of the character to making another actor, as a character, feel something (for example, *hopeful about our future together*), then you do not have to be concerned about whether or not you or your scene partner is living believably within the given circumstances. You do not have to be concerned about the future facts of the play or whether or not the character achieves his desires. By fully committing to action, you can live in the present moment as the character, setting about making your scene partner *feel* as a means toward achieving your objective.

This approach to action can help actors to focus on sources outside of themselves. Inexperienced actors and students learning how to act may be self-conscious. You may find yourself with a case of stage fright if you are, inadvertently, making the play about yourself, rather than serving the needs of the character and play as a whole. By placing your attention on sources outside of yourself through playing actions in order to achieve an objective, you have an organic and productive means of turning this inward-directed focus to the outside, where it can better serve the play.

QUESTIONS AND ANSWERS

1. **Question:** Is there a rule of thumb for playing action?
   Answer: In life, we affect one another's feelings naturally; we do not need to be taught how to do it. However, in acting we do need to be specific about whatever action we choose to play at a given moment. If you are not specific about your choice, your acting will be vague. The body is a remarkable instrument. Specifically playing an action allows you to commit yourself, in both body and mind, in accordance with that action. Lack of specificity can confuse the body, which can manifest as tension and a blockage of energy release.

2. **Question:** How do you make an object feel something?
   Answer: You cannot. It is the attempt to make the object feel that engages you. By committing yourself to making an object feel, for example, *important,* you engage yourself in an emotional way and create an emotional connection to the thing itself, as well as generating

an experience in the audience. It takes an act of the imagination to hold a prop meant to be a "gift" in your hands and connect with it in an emotional way. Perhaps you see in the gift the thought behind why your friend bought it for you or an image of her shopping for it. The more simply you can do this the more effective it will be. The point is to choose an action, consistant with an objective, and commit yourself to release that action on the source. Seemingly simple, it can be quite challenging to do so without bringing in mannerisms and affectations in order to "show" your audience your "acting." Ironically, the less you "perform" and the more you commit to actions, the better your acting will be.

3. **Question:** Doesn't it put you in your head to have to think: "Okay, I want to make her feel wrong" in the middle of a scene?
Answer: In a similar way to learning and recalling your lines while in rehearsal, when you are first beginning to work with a scene, you may have to recall what the action is and to think about releasing that action onto your scene partner. Ideally, with rehearsal and practice, like your remembered lines, your actions will become second nature and you will not have to think about them, but move directly into their execution.

4. **Question:** When first beginning to rehearse a role, once you decide on an objective, is it beneficial to plan your actions step-by-step at home and then execute them in rehearsal?
Answer: While you might jot a few words for action choices if inspiration strikes you on the bus or while making dinner, it is better to test and adjust your action choices within the natural context of a rehearsal.

As the scene unfolds in rehearsal several things could happen:

1. You may find that the action doesn't work for the objective. In that case, you can change it.

2. You may find that it works to a point, but somewhere in the scene you notice a change; a place where the scene shifts, perhaps the subject of the scene changes. This may be a place for a new action choice.

3. You may find that you change your action intuitively at some point. This is the time to make more detailed notes. When you have finished the scene, think back to when it changed. You may not know exactly what the action choice was, but you feel that it was a choice that worked. This can be a very productive way of working, because your intuition is becoming your guide. Then, upon reflection, you can articulate what you have been doing by asking yourself, "What action was I playing at that moment that seemed to work so well?" Further, "What was the source of my changing the initial action to the new action?" Try to articulate the change; to define what change

occurred in terms of a specific action. When you determine what it is, make a simple pencil note in the margin of your script, such as "guilty." In this way you will be able to repeat it time after time. Likewise, you can play with the how of guilty, such as "gently." There too, in your script, you would notate that as a reminder. Eventually your script becomes obsolete, as you remember your lines and the actions, as well as the hows of the actions, all become second nature to you.

5. **Question:** Will I have to do the work of defining actions and the hows of the actions throughout my career?

Answer: The more you do the work when first learning and experimenting with this way of approaching a role, the less you will need to do later on in your career, as this way of working becomes second nature to you. You may find yourself simply thinking about your actions and the hows of the actions automatically, as part of what you do; intuitively incorporating the approach into your rehearsal process. But it takes time to make this way of working habitual. The sooner you start working this way the more proficient you will become. However, like learning anything else, it takes discipline and practice. It requires you to let go of limiting habits you might bring to your work, such as indicating what a scene is about, rather than commiting yourself to achieving an objective through action.

Putting it all Together

THIS CHAPTER SHOWS HOW TO BEGIN APPLYING THIS method to a role. It starts with the step of reading the play three times as discussed in Chapter 1 followed by addressing the questions: *Who am I?, Where am I?* and *When am I there?*, and *What do I want?* (the super-objective). As insights are gained through these questions, the other questions—*What do I want?* (the objective), *How do I get what I want?*, and *What do I do if I get or don't get what I want?*—are applied, as they relate to scenes within the play. In most plays, many insights can be derived from addressing the questions and many possible "right" answers or conclusions can be determined. Each person, whether on stage or in the audience, will bring his own background to the theatre experience. That background and experience informs the way in which an individual understands the play and the performance. While this analysis does not show every conceivable answer to all of the questions, it demonstrates some ways in which important insights can be derived that lead to meaningful choices. Addressing the questions over time, through an actual rehearsal and production process, will yield many more insights than will this analysis.

Getting Started

Any play could serve as a model. This chapter shows how the methodology can be applied to the characters Nina and Treplev in *The Sea Gull.* By walking through this analysis, you can begin to create your personal structure for applying the methodology and, thereby, gain knowledge for applying it to other roles in other plays. Each and every role in any play will yield a different set of insights when the questions are addressed. Applying the question *Where am I?* will lead to different answers and, therefore, different choices; for example, playing Brick in *Cat on a Hot Tin Roof*, set indoors in Mississippi, versus Jerry in the *The Zoo Story*, set outside in Central Park, versus Lvov in Chekhov's *Ivanov*, set indoors and outdoors in Central Russia, versus Mae in *Fool For Love*, set in a motel in the Mohave Desert.

This sample application is not about how to act Chekhov's plays per se, nor is it a detailed analysis of this play from a critical standpoint. This is a sample application to demonstrate how an actor might begin to glean insights, make choices, and begin to structure those choices for acting the role. As you read through this chapter, imagine you have been cast as either Nina or Treplev and are examining the role for rehearsal and performance. (For a refresher on the detailed suggestions on a purposeful way to read through a play three times and in three different ways, you might want to consult the outline given in Chapter 1.

First Reading

Keep in mind from earlier chapters that the importance of this first reading is a way to gain an overall impression and familiarity with the play, and what experiences and impressions an audience member might have. The following character list and synopsis are provided for the convenience of the reader who is unfamiliar with *The Sea Gull*. You will find it very helpful to read the full play yourself, if you have not already done so.

The major characters include:

Treplev: A young man who aspires to be a writer. Irina is his mother. He is in love with Nina.

Nina: An aspiring actress who lives in the nearby estate across the lake. (Though the preferred term today would be "actor," both Chekhov and the characters in the play refer to Nina and Irina as "actress" so that is the term used here.)

Irina: A famous actress, Treplev's mother and Trigorin's lover.

Trigorin: a famous writer and Irina's lover.

Masha: A woman in love with Treplev.

Medvendenko: A school teacher, in love with Masha. Masha and Medvendenko marry in the course of the play.

Doctor Dorn: A local physician.

Act I

Irina and Trigorin are on vacation and have come to visit the estate where the play is set. All of the characters gather to watch Nina perform in a play written by Treplev. During the performance (a long monologue performed by Nina), Irina makes fun of Treplev's writing, and Treplev ends the performance prematurely and disappears into the woods surrounding the estate. Masha chases after him. Masha returns unable to find Treplev. She confesses to Dorn her love of Treplev. He can offer no consolation because he knows that Treplev loves Nina. Dorn, the only audience member who liked the play, praises Treplev for his work. Treplev, appreciative, exits in tears looking for Nina.

Act II

Act II takes place several days later on the lawn of the estate. Treplev appears with a dead sea gull, which he shot, and offers it to Nina as a symbol of his own fate: he will shoot himself, too, because she has withdrawn her love. They quarrel. Treplev exits as Trigorin enters. Nina and Trigorin have a long scene in which he discusses his life as a writer, and she declares that she would love to become a famous actress. The conversation is disrupted by Irina who says that she and Trigorin will be extending their stay at the estate.

Act III

Act III takes place in the dining room of Sorin's estate one week after the end of Act II. Sometime after Act I, Treplev challenged Trigorin to a duel over Nina, but Trigorin refused to participate. Treplev has a minor head wound from a failed suicide attempt. Trigorin asks Irina if both he and she can remain on the estate a while longer. Irina, aware of Trigorin's growing attraction to Nina, refuses. As they are leaving, Nina covertly informs Trigorin that she is running away to Moscow to become an actress. He gives her the name of his hotel in Moscow and they kiss.

Act IV

Act IV takes place in Treplev's study at the estate over two years after Act III. Although Masha has married, she still loves Treplev. It is disclosed that an affair between Nina and Trigorin led to Nina having a child, now deceased. Afterwards, Trigorin returned to Irina. Events have brought everyone back to the estate. Irina arrives accompanied by Trigorin. Treplev and Trigorin shake hands and "make up." Everyone except Treplev retires to another room. Nina enters and confesses to

Treplev that she still loves Trigorin. Then she says goodbye and leaves. Treplev tears up all of his manuscripts and burns them, exits, and kills himself with a pistol. Dr. Dorn discovers the body, but tells everyone that the noise was due to a bottle exploding in his medicine bag. He then pulls Trigorin aside, explains what has happened, and asks him to take Irina away.

First Impressions

In reading *The Sea Gull*, you will find that it is set on a beautiful estate on a lake over a two-year period at the turn of the twentieth century. It is about love and art and how people sometimes confuse the two elements. It is about acting and being an actress, writing and being a playwright. It is about pursuing people who are not good for us and ignoring those who are. The play focuses on the lives of family members and friends. Relationships that were at one time loving become disrupted as new infatuations enter their lives. It examines the need for our work to be validated by others, particularly those we admire. Treplev takes his own life (Why? to punish Nina? Because his work is not respected? Because he can't live without Nina's love?). Nina is determined to become a successful, working actress, seemingly, at all costs (Why? Because she is an artist and must work?). There is more to savor in the first reading, but this is enough to start.

Second Reading

This reading is where you identify the facts and collect specific information about the who, where, and when of the play. Let these facts become jumping off points for your imagination. In *The Sea Gull*, Act I takes place outdoors by the lake. Treplev writes plays and wants to be published. He is the son of a shopkeeper from Kiev and has very little money. Once you understand the fact that you, as Treplev, wrote a play that is about to be performed in front of your mother, a famous actress, and Trigorin, a famous writer, you can begin to imagine what this means—perhaps the anticipation of failure or success, perhaps the anticipation that something might go wrong, drives you to make sure everything is prepared, which can lead to physical activities, such as arranging a bench and pulling a curtain tight.

Facts for Nina include that she acts in Treplev's play and wants to be a famous actress. She lives on an estate on the other side of the lake. She has an affair with Trigorin. To say that Nina is anxious is not a fact, but an assessment of her condition. There is no doctor's note or psychologist's evaluation cited in the text to prove that she is anxious, although you, as Nina, could decide that she is anxious. This is a strong choice that seems logical under the given circumstances: that she is about to perform in front of a famous writer and actress. It is important to draw a distinction between the choice that she is anxious and the fact that she will shortly perform. As Nina, when you understand the fact that a famous writer and actress are coming to see you perform you can choose the objective that you, as Nina, want *to get them to demonstrate admiration of you.*

You can see that facts are important in providing the groundwork for your imagination. From the facts you can begin to use your imagination to fully address the basic questions. Define the specific facts and be clear with yourself at which points you are making a reasonable, strong, and specific choice through using your imagination. You may need to make notes in your script, or you may be able to keep things clear in your mind. Allow your imagination to flourish during early readings, but be sure you understand the given circumstances and facts about the play as written. This can take time and will probably require you to draw some logical conclusions. Some actors find benefit in re-reading the play a number of times in this second reading phase in order to understand as many facts as possible.

Third Reading

It is crucial to begin to see and hear through the eyes and ears of the character as defined in the text. Practice saying "I" when referring to your character. Take care not to judge your character in a negative way, as it will distance you from emotionally identifying with the role. (In *The Three Sisters*, Natasha could be seen as domineering from the point of view of Olga, but in her own mind she is nervous, perhaps awkward, but she cares deeply for her children.) In *The Sea Gull*, while Treplev sees his mother, Irina, as cheap, Irina sees herself as thrifty. Treplev's concerns are different from Nina's, and, therefore, his way of perceiving differs. From his point of view, the beginning of Act I is about getting ready to stage his play. The love of his life, Nina, is going to act in the play. His mother, the famous actress, and her boyfriend, the famous writer, will be in the audience. From Treplev's point of view, they know the theatre and whether or not a play is well written. His desire to impress them will inform his actions in the early parts of the play.

After three readings of the play, you will have begun to understand the story from the point of view of the character. You can address the central questions, referring back to the play, and using your imagination to fill in information not stated in the dialogue or notes. Remember that in keeping with the idea of living truthfully, you must ignore the fact that you know Treplev never succeeds in his desires. Remember: do not bring the knowledge of what is going to happen to the character to bear on the playing of the role from moment to moment, as it will have a detrimental affect on your performance. Why would any character pursue a desire that he knows would never be achieved?

The Questions

Ask the questions:

> *Who am I?*
> *Where am I? and When am I there?*
> *What do I want?*
> *How do I get what I want?*
> *What do I do if I get or don't get what I want?*

In applying the questions, your knowledge of the story, the given circumstances, and the point of view of Nina or Treplev will increase. Some of the information pertaining to *Where am I? and When am I there?* will have been discovered when you read the play for understanding the facts. However, what those facts about times and places mean to Treplev and Nina differ depending on a number of factors, including what it is they want. Addressing one question will lead to insights for addressing other questions. This analysis begins below with trust that in being given a role you will take your analysis further and deeper for that specific role and play.

The Title

The title of a play is meaningful.

Ask yourself: *What significance is a sea gull to my Who am I?*

Nina: I call myself a sea gull, but only *after* Treplev has laid a dead sea gull at my feet.

Perhaps Nina feels like a beautiful, free bird that that could be "killed" by a man? By Treplev, specifically? Is Treplev's demand for love "killing" her by holding her back? Is she trying to fly free for her art, but Treplev's expectations are holding her back?

Treplev: I shoot and kill a sea gull and lay it at Nina's feet before she begins to refer to herself as one.

Does it show how powerful his love is; that he would kill for her (or die for her)? Is it a gift? Is it significant because it shows he is willing to kill something? (Eventually, himself.) Is the sea gull "Nina" to Treplev? Does he want to hold onto her at any cost?

Who am I?

In Chapter 1, some categories for examining the question are introduced. In this example analysis, only categories relevant to *The Sea Gull* and Treplev and Nina are examined with much detail.

In addressing the question, *Who am I?*, first look to the play and then use your imagination. In the Robert W. Corrigan translation of *The Sea Gull*, the cast list at the beginning of the play offers scant details, stating that Treplev is the "son of Irina," an "actress," and that Nina is "a young girl, daughter of a wealthy landowner." More information must be found in the play itself, beginning with careful readings.

You can begin to define the *Who am I?* for both Nina and Treplev by looking at some of the lines. For example, in Act I Treplev questions his identity and purpose in life in a most revealing way. Early in Act I he says:

"Uncle, can you imagine anything more impossible, more hopeless, than to be alone—a nonentity—in a room full of celebrities, writers, and actors and know that you were being tolerated only because you were her son? Who am I? What am I? I left the University at the end of my junior year due to 'circumstances,' as our editors put it, 'over which we have no control.' I haven't any talent, no money, and I'm described on my passport as a shopkeeper from Kiev."

In the monologue, you, as Treplev, can begin to define the relationship Treplev has with his mother. You can begin to define why Treplev decides to become a writer. The text indicates that by Act IV you have attained some degree of success as a writer, despite the self-assessment that you have no talent. It is presumed that your father either walked out or he is dead. It is likely that Irina left you, as a child, with your uncle Sorin and others when she toured. A strong bond could have developed between you and Sorin, and there is much evidence in the text to support this conclusion. You, as Treplev, could make the choice that the reason for your frankness and openness in the above is that there are intimacy and trust between you. Conversely, the ambivalence in your feelings toward your mother can affect the way in which you interact. The two major scenes in which you appear with your mother end in arguments. Using these beginnings as jumping off points, you could construct a detailed picture of the *Who am I?* for Treplev, Nina, or any character in any play.

Fictional Or Real?

Ask yourself: *Is my character fictional or based on a real person?*

Nina: Fictional. There are no indications in the play that she is based on a real person from history. There is no documentation that such a person existed.

Treplev: Fictional. There are no indications in the play that he is based on a real person from history. There is no documentation that such a person existed.

Three-Dimensional Or Stereotype?

Ask yourself: *Is my character a stereotype or a three-dimensional character? Remember: a three-dimensional character has a unique persona; while a stereotype is drawn with a broader brush and has traits society recognizes as typical.*

Nina: Three-dimensional. While elements of her personality can be recognized in young women who wish for a stage career, such as the desire to become a "star," there is nothing in the play to indicate that she is based on a stereotype.

Treplev: Three-dimensional. There are elements of his personality that can be recognized in other young men who wish to be admired, respected, and successful in their chosen career, but there is nothing in the play to indicate that he is a stereotype.

Passions (Likes, Dislikes, Loves, And Hates)

Nina Narrative: I love the theatre and the lifestyle that goes along with it. I greatly admire Irina as a famous actress and Trigorin as a famous writer. I long for a career in the theatre. Importantly, I declare to Trigorin that I would love to be famous. My desire to become an actress is not just a fantasy. I run away from home, leaving Treplev, family, and friends to move to Moscow to become an actress. I must consider whether or not I love Treplev.

The choice that Nina was at one time in love with Treplev can be observed by the way in which he reacts to her when she withdraw myself from him, first revealed fully in Act II. As Nina, you must make a distinction between loving and being in love with someone, because this distinction is crucial in defining how Nina interacts with Treplev and Trigorin. In playing the role you, as Nina, might make the distinction that although you have begun to fall in love with Trigorin, you do not fully realize it. Consider that by falling in love with Trigorin, you are already on the path of withdrawing romantic love from Treplev. Yet you still care about him, as you return in Act IV to see him. These distinctions can inform choices about the way in which the scene might unfold.

Treplev Narrative: My background is different from Nina's. As a child I was surrounded by friends and associates of my mother. Many of these people were connected with the arts, particularly theatre and dance. I was fully aware of my mother's status as a celebrity. I desire to write "new forms" of plays. I wish to transform the theatre because to me it has grown stale. It could be argued that my desire to change the theatre is a way of rebelling against my mother, but I think that the plays she acts in are dull and meaningless. In any case, I am passionate about writing. I am also passionate about Nina. It is my love of Nina that compels me to express myself in destructive ways when she begins to reject me. I believe that she truly loves me and has gotten sidetrackesd by Trigorin and the excitement of being in the theatre.

If you are playing Treplev, you may consider that his love for Nina turns to hate at times throughout the play.

Body: Age

Ask yourself: *How old is my character at the start of the play? How much time passes from act to act, and, therefore, what changes occur in my age and in me, as a result?*

Nina Narrative: I have a father and a stepmother who keep a close watch over me. I am capable of running away to Moscow, giving birth to a child, and supporting myself as an actress. I am eighteen years old when I act in Treplev's play. I am twenty years old when Treplev kills himself. I have changed and I have struggled during the time since I left my parents and Treplev for Moscow. I am no longer the naive young girl that I was.

Nina's age is not specifically given, but she is defined as "a young girl, daughter-of-a-landowner." Trigorin surmises that she is 18 or 19 in Act II. It is clear from the text that more than two years pass over the time of the play.

> **Treplev Narrative:** I am 25 years old at the beginning of the play and I am 27 when Nina returns, two years later.

Body: Movement

Ask yourself: *How might my body movements be affected by my age or other aspects of my character and personality?*

> **Nina Narrative:** I identify with a sea gull. In what way might an image of a sea gull inform my movement?
>
> **Treplev Narrative:** I feel the weight of the world on my shoulders. I get depressed, which manifests as a sunken chest.

Relationships

Ask yourself: *What are my relationships to the other characters in the play? Below are some examples, but there are many more to be defined.*

> **Nina Narrative:** My parents do not appear in the play. However, they exert influence over me, as I need to be home before it gets dark. I am worried about my father and stepmother. My parents are wealthy, but I don't know how much money we have. Like Treplev's mother, my father is stingy. Treplev and I are boyfriend/ girlfriend at the start of the play. However, we do not see the relationship in the same way.
>
> **Treplev Narrative:** My father either walked out on us or he is dead. My mother is very much alive. While I love her, there are things about her that I dislike. I call her "stingy" when she refuses to help finance medical expenses for her brother. Considering my relationship with Trigorin: I am jealous of him, due to his success as a writer and becoming the apple of Nina's eye. I challenge him to a duel, and I attempt (and eventually commit) suicide. My most

significant relationship is with Nina. It is clear that Nina was in love with me at one time. However, her love for me diminishes as the play progresses. I must have her back at all costs.

As Treplev, you know part way through the play that Trigorin has an affair with Nina. These circumstances must be considered in determining how much you dislike or possibly hate Trigorin at different points in the play.

Relationships: Status

Social status is always important to an individual and would be important to Chekhov's characters. Status can be influenced by many factors, including birthright, education, ambition, and the type of job one holds.

Ask yourself: *Is status an important element in the play? Is my character of higher or lower status than the other character(s) with whom I share a scene? Does my status change in the play?*

Nina Narrative: I am "the daughter of a wealthy landowner," which gives me a higher level of status than ordinary workers. I wish to be a famous actress, like Irina, which would be an elevation of my current status. Although I am young and inexperienced at the beginning of the play, I mature and learn important "life lessons" over the two-year period in which the play takes place. A driving force in determining who I am lies in my desire to be a successful and famous actress.

Treplev Narrative: I am a struggling writer and uncomfortable financially. I am unsettled by my status as "the son of a famous actress," and I wish to better myself through my own success as an author. To publish and be produced is in part what I desire most in life. This would elevate me in the eyes of my mother and Nina. My birth certificate reads, "Son of a shopkeeper from Kiev." My mother is famous, and my Uncle's estate elevates my status. I attended a university, but left "due to circumstances beyond my control." (Those circumstances are not revealed in the play.)

This is an excellent opportunity to use your imagination to flesh out the details of Treplev's "circumstances" for leaving the university, as you will play him. Were you expelled for cheating? Caught with Nina in your room after hours? Caught with someone else in your room? Did you spend all your time writing plays and end up failing your courses? Cursed a professor who didn't see your brilliance? This is an opportunity to practice playing and strengthening your imagination. For example, due to several comments throughout the play regarding Irina and money, it is likely that you simply could not afford to continue to attend the university. Consider the fact that you have been wearing the same worn-out jacket for a very long time. Sorin asks Irina to give you some money and she refuses with: *I haven't got the money.* [Sorin laughs] *Well I don't.*

Relationship: Race, Culture, And Place Of Origin

Ask yourself: *Are my character's race, culture, and/or place of origin significant?*

> **Nina:** While *The Sea Gull* takes place in Russia, Chekhov's writing focuses on universal human needs and wants, such as love, career, and family.
>
> There is no indication that race, culture or place of origin are meant to be specifically influential within the play.
>
> **Treplev:** While *The Sea Gull* takes place in Russia, Chekhov's writing focuses on universal human needs and wants, such as love, career, and family.
>
> There is no indication that race, culture or place of origin are meant to be specifically influential within the play.

Where am I?

Though you will usually focus on *Where am I?* from a single character's point of view, it is important to remember that the same place will have different meanings for different characters.

> **Nina Narrative:** I live next to an estate in Russia that is visited by a famous professional actress and an equally famous writer. I cannot fulfill my dream to be a famous actress if I continue to stay with my parents on an estate far from Moscow. I have the opportunity to perform for them because Treplev has written a play with me as its only character. Through this, I have the opportunity to know and perhaps learn from them.
>
> The *Where am I?* in Act II focuses on a lawn on Sorin's estate, from which the lake can be seen. For me, this place affords an opportunity

to meet Trigorin, alone. In Act III, Trigorin and I share a long kiss after Irina exits. The kiss takes place inside the house with servants and others around that might see us. This knowledge informs the way in which we deal with the kiss. In the final act, while Treplev is alone in this room when I enter, the others are in the next room. I do not want anyone except Treplev to know I am there.

> **Treplev Narrative:** This is "my" home. Though technically the house and land belong to my Uncle Sorin, I have spent much time here, and I consider it my home. I am more familiar and comfortable in the various locations than Nina is. The narrower *Where am I?* in Act II focuses on a lawn on Sorin's estate, from which the lake can be seen. The place has significant meaning to me in that it is the place where those people who are important to me will see my play performed. It has significance to me in that it is where Nina is at the time. It is also significant because it is where Trigorin will pass. In Act III, the dining room feels safe and provides some degree of intimacy to talk privately with my mother. In the final act, I am very much at home in the my study. The others, including Trigorin, are next door. I do not participate, but can hear them playing.

When am I There?

The play was written in 1895. However, aside from odd terms, such as "merchant lotharios," there is nothing specific in this play that reflects that time in history requires investigation, unless the designers and director determined that the production aesthetic would be strongly informed by it. A director could choose to set it in any time period. Once a time period choice has been made, you can investigate the period and understand the aesthetic of the production in order to make choices. However, the time that passes in and between acts is fixed and, therefore, is relevant to your analysis.

> **Nina Narrative:** The play opens in the early evening before nightfall when I am visiting Sorin's estate. It is significant to me because my father has told me to be home before dark. I need to finish the performance and be on my way or risk punishment. After the play, I have only a short amount of time to visit with Irina and Trigorin and the others. Act II takes place a few days later in the afternoon, on the day and near the time that Irina and Trigorin are to leave. It is also the time that Trigorin must return from fishing, walking past me in order to enter the estate. Act III takes place at a non-

specific time shortly after Act II,. I offer Trigorin a medallion with the words, "If ever you need my life, come and take it." Act IV takes place two years after the end of Act III. In the unseen internal between Acts III and IV, I ran away to Moscow, had an affair with Trigorin, became an actress, had a baby, and the baby died. I return to the estate at the time Irina and Trigorin are visiting, as well. However, I only visit Treplev.

Treplev Narrative: Act I is significant because my play is being staged in front of my mother, a famous actress, and her boyfriend, a famous writer and it is important to me that my work be well received. Act II is significant to me because I witness Nina's withdrawal from me. Though much of the change took place in the imaginary time between acts I and II, the change is evident through our dialogue. I accuse her of turning "cold" toward me; the implication is that there was a time when she was warmer. By Act III, I have attempted suicide. The attempt is directly related to Nina's withdrawal and her infatuation with Trigorin. The time between my last appearance in Act II and my scene in Act III is significant in that I have been observing Nina withdrawing more and more and moving closer and closer to Trigorin. Sometime after Act III and before Act IV, Nina runs away and has an affair with Trigorin. I know these things because I have been spying on Nina, as I reveal in Act IV. Meanwhile, my career as a writer is meeting with success. Act IV takes place in winter, two years later. I continue to write. Nina unexpectedly arrives to visit me. She leaves after a long scene. I kill myself.

It is important for the actor playing Treplev to examine imaginary time. You must recognize that you and Nina have a history together; a time when "I was happy" that Treplev refers to in Act IV. Therefore, the imaginary time before the play takes place has meaning for you, as Treplev. In playing Treplev, consider the changes you see in Nina, which came about between Acts 1 and II. For example, it is very likely that these changes you have been observing have not been going on for long, perhaps only since the arrival of Irina and, especially, Trigorin.

What Do I Want?

The super-objective states what a character wants from the beginning to the end of the play. The objectives lead toward the super-objective. The super-objective and all the objectives are chosen through an analysis of the role.

Super-Objective

Nina: To become a successful professional actress

This is just one example of a strong, playable super-objective. Use your answers to the first three questions to help to create Nina's super-objective. It is clear from the play that what is most important to Nina has to do with being an actress. You might think that "Becoming a professional actress" could be your super-objective. But you do become a professional actress sometime before Act IV. A better choice would be to *become a successful professional actress like Irina*. Once you choose a super-objective for Nina, you can analyze the scenes in which she appears and create objectives that relate to and help her accomplish her super-objective. Make *to become a professional actress* an *objective*, which supports the super-objective, *to become a successful professional actress*.

In Act III, you have a long scene with Trigorin. You may choose to make that scene's objective *to get Trigorin to fall in love with me*. While the dialogue does not specifically indicate that is what the scene is about, the events following it (your kiss, your covert message to him, your secret meeting, your affair, and your pregnancy) support the choice for that particular objective. More importantly, this objective could serve your super-objective (*to become a successful professional actress*) because Trigorin is a great writer who is from that "world" of which you long to become a part. Presumably, Trigorin has connections in Moscow.

Treplev: To share a love relationship and successful career with Nina

In formulating a super-objective for Treplev, recognize that he wants to become a successful writer. By the play's end he has attained some level of success, arguably more than Nina has. But when Nina leaves at the end of Act IV, she is returning to her theatre career to continue her pursuit of becoming a successful professional actress. You burn your manuscripts and kill yourself. When examining Treplev's likes, dislikes, loves, and hates through the question *Who am I?*, most actors find that Nina is the most important of Treplev's loves. As it appears that his suicide is directly related to Nina's rejection of him, rather than publishers rejecting his writing or some other reason; a strong choice for his super-objective would be to relate it to Nina in some way.

The super-objective, *to share a love relationship and successful career with Nina*, would be a good choice for the actor playing Treplev. This provides a context for creating an objective for the Nina/Treplev scene in Act II, such as *to get Nina to declare her love for me* or *to get Nina to behave toward me as she used to*, which serves the super-objective above. By shocking her with the dead sea gull, you can attempt to get her to start paying attention to you rather than to Trigorin.

Objectives

Nina: There will be many objectives for me as I move through the play.

One possible set of objectives is noted in the specific scene analysis a little further in this chapter. As an actor, you may find making notes in your script will help clarify your objective choices.

Treplev: There will be many objectives for me as I move through the play.

One possible set of objectives is noted in the specific scene analysis a little further in this chapter. As an actor, you may find making notes in your script will help clarify your objective choices.

How Do I Get What I Want?

What the actor must do in performance is both simple and difficult: fully commit to sending and receiving action. There are many ways to get someone to do something, but whatever the choice, it should be articulated in terms of making someone else feel something. The feeling can vary, so long as it is consistent with achieving the objective. You should not be thinking about *Who am I?* or *Where am I?* or *What do I want?* while acting, just as a wide receiver in football should not be thinking about how he formulated the pattern he is running while going out for a pass. The thinking work must be done prior to the performance.

Nina: There will be many action choices for me as I move through the play.

One possible set of action choices is noted in the specific scene analysis a little further in this chapter. As an actor, you may find making notes in your script will help clarify your choices.

Treplev: There will be many action choices for me as I move through the play.

One possible set of action choices is noted in the specific scene analysis a little further in this chapter. As an actor, you may find making notes in your script will help clarify your choices.

How of The Action

The *How* of the action can be a source of discovery. Use it to reveal a new side of the *Who am I?* or to focus or broaden an insight into your *Who am I?* You, as Treplev, may choose to make Nina feel loved *desperately.* Making this choice is directly related to the given circumstances of the play because Treplev kills himself in the end. Nina might make Treplev feel strange *stand-offishly.* By making Treplev feel strange *stand-offishly,* the actor playing Nina actually helps her scene partner by providing a source for his line "You're cold to me . . . " As Treplev, you might try to make your mother feel stupid *sarcastically,* as you suggest that her boyfriend is "cultivating Nina's potential" out in the garden. Sarcasm can be connected to Treplev's bitterness and jealousy towards Trigorin, who threatens Treplev's desire to make himself successful in the eyes of those who love him.

At the end of Act I, Masha painfully confesses her love for Treplev to Doctor Dorn. The actor playing Dorn may choose *to make Masha feel consoled* in a *fatherly* way, as close readings of the play suggest that she is his illegitimate daughter. The important point to focus on, when deciding how an action is played, is that it must somehow relate to the way in which your character has been defined through the major questions, the given circumstances, and what you are receiving from the other actor, as character, in the heat of the moment.

Nina: There will be many "How of the action" choices for me as I move through the play.

One possible set of action choices is noted in the specific scene analysis a little further in this chapter. As an actor, you may find making notes in your script will help clarify your choices.

Treplev: There will be many "how of the action" choices for me as I move through the play.

One possible set of action choices is noted in the specific scene analysis a little further in this chapter. As an actor, you may find making notes in your script will help clarify your choices.

What Do I Do After I Get or Fail to Get What I Want?

Remember that objectives are something you create on behalf of the character. Sometimes the characters will achieve his objective in the course of the scene, at which point a new objective can be pursued.

Sometimes you may discover partway through a scene that you are not going to get what you want, so you will shift to a new objective. Often times the playwright has the character exit after achieving or failing to achieve a given objective, and you will have moment to catch your breath before beginning a new scene with a new objective.

Nina: There are many choices to decide what to do after I get (or don't get) what I want, as I move through the play.

One possible set of choices is noted in the specific scene analysis further ahead in this chapter. As an actor, you may find making notes in your script will help clarify your choices.

Treplev: There are many choices to decide what to do after I get (or don't get) what I want, as I move through the play.

One possible set of choices is noted in the specific scene analysis further ahead in this chapter. As an actor, you may find making notes in your script will help clarify your choices.

Using This Approach To Analyze A Scene

Now that you, thinking as an actor cast as either Nina or Treplev, have finished reading the play a number of times, and made many observations about both the play as a whole and your specific role, it is time to practice focusing on a specific scene. You will ask the same questions, but things will change more quickly in many instances (and more slowly in others) as some of the "big picture" facts may not change, though the smaller details will still benefit from examination.

The Text to be Analyzed: *The Sea Gull* by Anton Chekhov, Act II, Nina and Treplev

Nina's Soliloquy Before The Scene Begins

NINA: [*alone*] How strange it is to see a famous actress crying . . . and over nothing! And isn't it strange that a famous writer spends all his time fishing? Here he is, a best seller, written about in all the papers, his pictures everywhere, his books translated into foreign languages, and . . . he gets all excited if he catches a couple of perch. I always thought that famous people were proud and aloof and that they despised the crowd; I thought they used their glory and fame to get revenge on people who put wealth and position above everything else. But here they are crying, and fishing, and playing cards, and laughing and getting upset like everyone else.

Treplev's Entrance Disrupting Nina

TREPLEV: [*Enters, carrying a gun and a dead sea gull.*] Are you all alone?

NINA: Yes. [*Treplev lays the sea gull at her feet.*] What does this mean?

TREPLEV: I was rotten enough to kill this sea gull today. I lay it at your feet.

NINA: What's wrong with you? [*Picks up the sea gull and looks at it.*]

TREPLEV: [*after a pause*] And soon I'm going to kill myself in the same way.

NINA: What is wrong with you? This isn't like you at all!

TREPLEV: That's true! I began to change when you did. You've changed towards me and you know it . . . You're cold to me, and my very presence bothers you.

NINA: You've been so irritable lately, and most of the time you talk in riddles, and I don't understand a word you're saying. And I suppose now that this sea gull, here, is some kind of symbol, too. Well, forgive me, I don't understand that, either . . . [*Putting the sea gull on the seat.*] I'm too simple minded to understand you.

Treplev's Short Monologue At The End Of The Scene

TREPLEV: It all began the night my play failed. Women never forgive failure. Well, I burnt it! Every bit of it! Oh, if you only knew how unhappy I am! And the way you've rejected me, I can't understand it! . . . It's as if I woke up one morning and found the lake suddenly drying up. You said that you're too simple minded to understand me. Tell me, what's there to understand? Nobody liked my play, so now you despise my talent, and think I'm ordinary and insignificant, like all the rest of them . . . [*Stamping his foot.*] Oh, how well I understand. How well! It's like a nail in my head . . . Oh, damn it . . . And my pride . . . sucking my life blood . . . like a snake . . . [*Sees Trigorin, who enters reading.*] But here comes the real genius, he walks like Hamlet himself, and with a book, too. [*Mimics.*] "Words, words, words." . . . The sun has hardly touched you and already you're smiling and your eyes are melting in its rays. I won't bother you any more . . . [*Goes out quickly.*]

Nina: Who am I?

I am beginning to withdraw from Treplev and look toward a future in the theatre as an accomplished actress—a future that does not include him.

The question of an overall *Who am I?* for Nina has been examined. In this scene from Act II, her *Who am I?* has shifted, as Treplev points out with the line *"you've changed towards me—."*

Nina: Where Am I And When Am I There?

I am standing on the lawn of the estate, specifically, at a point where I can see the path Trigorin would take, should he happen to walk back from fishing.

Address the specifics of this question in every scene that you, as Nina, appear in. To define the place in terms of a lawn on the estate, while true, does not reveal enough about what the place means to you, as Nina, in this particular time. Why do you stand alone on the lawn with a clear view of the lake? A strong choice is that you wish to see Trigorin. As you live on the other side of the lake, you could very well observe Trigorin fishing at a particular time each day. By knowing where he fishes and when he returns to the estate for dinner, you can conveniently position yourself between the estate and the lake in order to "accidentally" run into him.

For the actor playing Nina, choosing to observe Trigorin fishing, in her imagination, can help create the imaginary circumstances around the apparently innocuous meeting. (Importantly, the actor playing Treplev can imagine that this is what Nina is conspiring to do as well. Thus, he, too, shows up in the same location with the dead sea gull in order to intervene and make a bold, symbolic, and dangerous statement: "I will kill myself in the same way.")

Nina: What Do I Want?

One strong choice is that you are waiting to see Trigorin, as you wish to be alone with him in order to get him to fall in love with you. Another possibility is that you want to get him to befriend you. Both of these objectives can serve the super-objective: to become a successful, famous actress.

Obstacles:

1. I already have a boyfriend (Treplev).
2. Trigorin (the object of my love) already has a girlfriend (Treplev's mother).

3. Why would someone as famous and talented as Trigorin find me interesting?
4. If Treplev shows up, he will be in the way of my being alone with Trigorin? Also, Irina could find out that I am waiting around to meet with Trigorin.
5. Trigorin is leaving later that day for Moscow. (Although the plans change and they end up staying, you the actor know this, yet Nina does not. As far as Nina is concerned, this may be her only chance to be alone with Trigorin, ever.)

Stakes:

1. Without Trigorin's support, I might never be able to break into an acting career.

Beat 1

Transition 1: [Polina and Dorn exit.]
Source/Focus 1: Image of Irina, downstage right, whining. ("See" the image even before sending the action and speaking the line.)
Action: To make her feel childish.
How: Disapprovingly.

NINA: [*Alone*] How strange it is to see a famous actress crying . . . and over nothing!

Commentary: You, as Nina, can begin the action of making Irina feel childish immediately, before the line itself. You do not need lines in order to play action.

Beat 2

Source/Focus: Image of Trigorin, down left, standing knee-deep in the lake with pants rolled up, fishing.
Action: To make him feel childish.
How: Curiously.

NINA: And isn't it strange that a famous writer spends all his time fishing.

Commentary: Here the choice of "curiously" is connected to the fascination with Trigorin. Nina later has an affair with him, so it is reasonable that the "how" of the action is different from that used on Irina, although both of the actions are the same. It is significant that you have a view of the lake, as indicated in the play. Use your imagination to see an image of this lake with Trigorin on shore fishing. You might envision it in whatever logical direction from which Trigorin would later make his entrance.

Beat 3

Source/Focus: Newspaper page with a photo of Trigorin about three feet slightly down right and five feet off of the stage floor. Headline reads that his recent play is a best seller.

Action: To make him feel desired.

How: Affectionately

NINA: Here he is, a best seller, written about in all the papers, his pictures everywhere, his books translated into foreign languages, and . . . he gets all excited if he catches a couple of perch.

Commentary: Other images can work, so long as it affects you in some way. Perhaps an image of Trigorin fishing? The images help produce the experience that Nina is going through in this time and place. She is recognizing that, in a curious way, Irina and Trigorin, though famous, are just like anyone else she knows. You might find that an image of Trigorin being applauded by an audience, juxtaposed with him slipping and falling in the water as he fishes, will work for you.

Beat 4

Source/Focus: Irina arguing with Shamraev (manager of the estate), where the argument occurred earlier in the act, if doing the actual play. If not, in a place that opens you, as Nina, up to the audience, so that the audience "sees" what you "see."

Action: To make Irina feel petty.

How: Critically.

NINA: I always thought that famous people were proud and aloof and that they despised the crowd; I thought they used their glory and fame to get revenge on people who put wealth and position above everything else. But here they are crying, and fishing, and playing cards, and laughing, and getting upset like everyone else.

Commentary: Images of Irina being praised can be juxtaposed with her engaged in a petty argument with the manager of the estate.

The Scene Between Nina And Treplev
Personalization and Preparation for Nina

The next lines deal with the interaction between Nina and Treplev. If your objective as Nina is to get Trigorin to fall in love with you, things change for you with Treplev's entrance. Time has a new immediacy, as you anticipate Trigorin's arrival while dealing with Treplev. Unless

Treplev leaves, the *Where am I?* is no longer a place to be alone with Trigorin.

Nina's emotional experience at the start of the scene is optimistic and excited. The soliloquy reveals that she is in a state of wonder and curiosity about the world. In the soliloquy Nina discovers that Irina and Trigorin are just like everyone else. If you examine this in light of her super-objective, it is logical to assume that she now sees that fulfilling her dreams may not be as difficult to her as she previously thought. Allow the soliloquy to lead you into an appropriate emotional state.

Personalization and Preparation for Treplev

In playing Treplev you have time off-stage to prepare for your entrance by getting yourself into the appropriate emotional state of being. Consider Treplev's emotional experience when he enters. You are jealous of Nina's infatuation with Trigorin, and you are angry about your "failure" the night you staged your play. Something new is going on with Nina, and you are sensitive to it. You fear that Nina has "changed toward me." You have shot a sea gull, and you threaten to kill yourself. Consider where you are coming from when you enter with the dead sea gull. Presumably you have not been walking around for days with the dead bird, but killed it sometime earlier that day. Be specific in your imagination as to where and when the shooting occurred. You might also imagine that you considered shooting Trigorin, but killed the sea gull instead. As the actor, recognizing Treplev's potential for violence can help your process of understanding his emotional state.

In recognizing that Treplev is deeply troubled, you can begin to imagine the circumstances that lead to such intense jealousy and anger. As Treplev, you may strongly suspect that Nina is in this particular place in order to meet Trigorin. You can imagine, as Treplev would, the worst: that Nina has fallen out of love with you and is in love with Trigorin, confirming your suspicion that she has changed. You are resentful. You feel angry you were treated unfairly by your mother and now Nina. You do not feel that you deserve such treatment. You feel that your play was groundbreaking, and yet your mother made fun of it. You want to get even or hurt back. You have acted violently on a sea gull, and you plan to lay it at Nina's feet to warn her. As Treplev, begin to arouse yourself emotionally through your imagination, to fill in what happens between Acts I and II. Imagine that you and Nina have a picnic and all she does is talk about Trigorin. Imagine those things that trigger jealousy, anger, resentment, and the desire to retaliate. When Treplev enters, he is highly charged, upset, angry, and jealous.

Treplev: Who am I?

Although there is indication that Nina is beginning to change, Treplev's *Who am I?* has not changed, except in so far as her change is bringing out his anxiety.

Treplev: Where am I? *and* When am I there?

Although they are in the same place, somewhere on the lawn within view of the lake, this place is part of Treplev's home environment, while Nina is a visitor. It is clear from the text that Treplev is upset with Nina, and he feels that she has changed toward him. It is also clear that he is jealous about Trigorin. If playing Treplev, perhaps your choice is that you suspect that Nina is waiting for Trigorin, and, therefore, your *When am I there?* is significant in terms of anticipating Trigorin's arrival and watching for Nina's reaction to him. It is possible that Treplev is aware that Nina observes Trigorin's habits. It is probable that he has been spying on Nina. These habits are directly related imaginatively to the places in which they occur, and they should be considered when addressing the question, *Where am I?* and *When am I There?*

Treplev: **What do I want?**

The super-objective *to share a love relationship and a successful career in the theatre with Nina* would be a good choice for the actor playing Treplev overall. A good choice for Treplev's objective in this scene would be *to make Nina behave toward me as she used to,* as the objective almost always relates to something one character wants from another. Another equally valid choice that supports achievement of the super-objective is *to get Nina to demonstrate loyalty to me.* While it is possible the actor playing Treplev could choose as his objective *to get Nina to dislike Trigorin,* this choice is not as effective as a direct, positive one (*to get Nina to behave toward me as she used to*). By making and fulfilling strong choices, your performance will have specificity rather than general or vague expression.

A Note About Transitions

Transitions occur when there is an entrance or exit. In this scene, Treplev's entrance is a transition, and it brings with it a change in objectives. Caution should be used so as not to telegraph to the audience that there is a transition. Instead allow yourself to be influenced by outside sources that shift your focus, and with that shift in focus, allow the new objective (consistent with your super-objective) to emerge. In this scene, from Nina's point of view, the new situation is Treplev, whose entrance appears as an intrusion. Importantly, this would not have been the case earlier in the play, but from Nina's point of view, as her own *Who am I?* has changed, so, too, has her view of Treplev, as you can see by her lines, "You've been so irritable lately." Your negative reaction to him affects how he perceives you, which informs how he treats you, which informs how you perceive him, which informs how you treat him. Ideally, find a way to use the actions and reactions to build the intensity of the scene. At this particular time in the play, it would be useful to you, in playing Nina, to find something particularly unattractive about Treplev, such as his irritability.

Treplev's Objective: To get Nina to behave toward me as she used to.
Treplev's Obstacle: Nina views him as a failed playwright and Trigorin as a successful playwright.
Treplev's Stakes: His lack of success in comparison with Trigorin's could push Nina further away.

Nina's Objective: You might consider the objective *to make Treplev go away* as a possible choice that serves her super-objective, because she cannot very well get Trigorin to fall in love with her with Treplev "hanging around" with a dead sea gull and a shotgun.
Nina's Obstacle: She is still in a boyfriend/girlfriend relationship, and Treplev clearly wants something that must be dealt with.
Nina's Stakes: With Treplev there, she has no chance of being alone with Trigorin. At this time in the play Trigorin and Irina will soon be leaving for Moscow. This may be Nina's only chance of being alone with Trigorin.

Commentary: In the outline below, assume that each action choice that has been assigned to Nina and Treplev is played by that character throughout until the next action change the character has. Therefore, there is always an action defining and being played in each and every moment. This is true for the soliloquy, the scene, and the monologue. When do you, as Nina, notice Treplev? When you do, your objective, *to get Treplev to go away*, needs to operate through action. If you want Treplev to go away, how might you make him feel as a first choice? How about simply, *unwanted*? You, as Nina, do not need lines in order to make the actor, as Treplev, feel unwanted.

You can immediately begin to make him feel unwanted as soon as you see him.

Transition: Treplev Enters.

TREPLEV: [*Enters, carrying a gun and a dead sea gull.*]

Treplev's Focus/Source: Nina, specifically her negative attitude toward him.
Treplev's Action: To make her feel guilty.
Treplev's How: Dejectedly.
Treplev's Activity/Blocking: Enters, carrying gun and dead sea gull. Let's imagine that the actor playing Nina is standing center stage and that the blocking calls for Treplev to enter from off right and stand stage right. The actor playing Treplev should play the action: to make Nina feel guilty, immediately upon entering, not just when he has lines. Therefore, there can be a moment before Treplev's line when Treplev is standing stage right, simply making Nina feel guilty. Then:

TREPLEV: Are you all alone?

A Note Specific to Nina: What do you want? Nina's objective changes from *to get Trigorin to fall in love with me* to *to make Treplev go away*. Using the objective as a guide, the actor playing Nina may consider that when Treplev enters in the scene, she does not expect him. This is a strong choice because it creates drama through the shock of being confronted by her *ex*-boyfriend (depending on the actor playing Nina's decision about the status of their relationship at this particular time) with a dead sea gull and a gun. It is crucially important that you, as Nina, be vulnerable to Treplev and the reverse. This vulnerability includes how you receive what is being given to you by the other actor as character.

If Nina is there in hopes of having a private conversation with Trigorin, because this may be her only chance to do so before he and Irina leave for Moscow, this desire should inform the way in which you, as Nina, react to Treplev when he enters. When Treplev says, "Are you all alone?" can you, as Nina, allow Treplev to startle you with his line? So, perhaps you do not so much immediately understand the question Treplev asks, but are first startled out of your action, which was suggested above as to make Irina feel petty, played on the image of Irina arguing with Shamraev. Then, when you become fully aware of Treplev, you observe, listen, and feel his presence as you play your action and the how of the action from the point of view of your objective, which is to get him to leave. From that point of view, you can immediately play an action on him, such as to make him feel unwanted, and do so rudely.

Nina's Focus/Source: Treplev, strangely looking at her.
Nina's Action: To make him feel unwanted.
Nina's How: Rudely.
Commentary: The longer that Treplev stays in the area the greater the possibility that he will ruin Nina's chance to be alone with Trigorin, if Trigorin passes by. This insight is connected to asking the question, *When am I there?*

NINA: Yes. [*Treplev lays the sea gull at her feet.*]
Commentary: It is important for the actor playing Treplev to make a distinction between playing an action and the physical business of laying the sea gull at Nina's feet. Be specific in distinguishing *activities* from *actions*. Although Treplev must lay the sea gull at Nina's feet as indicated in the stage directions, you should not stop playing the *action* (in this case *to make Nina feel guilty*) because of that *activity*. Continue to play actions while simultaneously conducting any activities the script requires. In fact, the activity itself (in this instance, laying the bird at Nina's feet) should include the action and the how of the action. You, as Treplev, might choose to lay the bird at Nina's feet *ceremoniously*, while making her feel guilty. Laying it at her feet *ceremoniously* while playing the action to make her feel guilty is a strong choice. Giving yourself over totally to the action, the how of the action, the activity, and being vulnerable to the actor as Nina goes a long way toward living truthfully within the imaginary circumstances of the play.

Nina's Focus/Source: The sea gull.
Nina's Action: To make Treplev feel strange.
Nina's How: Disgustedly.
Commentary: As Nina, consider what Treplev is doing. He is laying a bloody sea gull at your feet. How do you see the bird? Is it disgusting? Is it beautiful? In analyzing the scene and referring to the objective, to make Treplev go away, you might play an action on the dead bird such as to make it feel disgusting, while simultaneously

making Treplev feel disgusting. Although Nina's focus is on the sea gull, she can source the action off of the sea gull and into Treplev. You, as Nina, have made two strong choices before you have even spoken your first line: To make Treplev feel unwanted, then shifting to make both the bird and Treplev feel disgusting is a way of moving toward your objective, *to make him leave.*

NINA: What does this mean?

Commentary: You, as Treplev, should be sensitive to how Nina reacts. If you are working with an actor who does not play action in terms of making someone feel something, you can work towards receiving what she does in a way that makes you feel unwanted and respond accordingly. Consider how Treplev hears the line "What does this mean?" from Nina. Is Treplev expecting her to understand what the dead sea gull means? Does Treplev want to shock her? Does it shock her? If Nina sends the action *to make Treplev feel unwanted*, do you feel unwanted? Does this confirm that something about her has changed? Ask this: What is the action and how of the action that the actor as Nina is sending? How can I be vulnerable to it? Understand that it is not about you personally but about playing a character. The only reason that you, as Treplev, would change the action choice from making Nina feel guilty to something else is because the first choice is not working to accomplish your objective, *to get Nina to declare her love for me.* However, it is too early in the scene to determine this. Therefore, you, as Treplev, should continue to make her feel guilty. Also, keep in mind that the action and the how of it are not dependent on lines. You can make someone *feel wrong* without vocalizing or prior to vocalizing, if you do not have lines.

Beat 4

Treplev's Focus/Source: Nina.
Treplev's Action: To make her feel guilty.
Treplev's How: Nobly.

TREPLEV: I was rotten enough to kill this sea gull today. I lay it at your feet.

Commentary: How does Nina interpret Treplev's activity, lines, and action? A good way of understanding how your character hears and takes in what another character says and does is by examining what your character says in response. Nina's response line implies that something is wrong with Treplev.

Nina's Focus/Source: Shift from bird to Treplev, perceiving in him something "wrong."
Nina's Action: Continues to make Treplev feel strange.
How: Shifts from disgustedly to tentatively.

NINA: What's wrong with you?

Commentary: In continuing the analysis of the scene, assuming the two actors as the characters are playing the following: Nina, to make Treplev feel strange and Treplev, to make Nina feel guilty, the action should not change unless something happens to make it change. The most important reason you should change an action is because the one that you are using is not working. Remember that the play determines whether or not an objective is being or has been fulfilled. If Nina's objective is to get Treplev to go away, his final line "I won't bother you any more!" followed by his exit reveals that she has accomplished her objective. However, characters do not always get what they want. In the above scene, Treplev's objective (*to get Nina to behave toward me as she used to*) is not accomplished, as the lines indicate.

Nina's Focus/Source: The dead sea gull, specifically select something about the sea gull, such as the expression on its face.
Nina's Action: To make Treplev feel wrong.
Nina's How: Gently.

NINA: [*Picks up the sea gull and looks at it.*]

Commentary: The title of the play is *The Sea Gull*. Ask yourself (as either Treplev or Nina) what the significance of a sea gull is to you. What does it symbolize? How does it inform your *Who am I?* Although Nina has no line she can still play an action on Treplev. Think of sourcing it off of the sea gull and into the actor playing Treplev.

Treplev's Focus/Source: The sea gull.
Treplev's Action: To make Nina feel fear.
Treplev's How: Ominously.

TREPLEV: [*after a pause*]

Commentary: You, as Treplev, can begin to make Nina feel fear during the pause. As Treplev, knowing that the action to make her feel guilty is not accomplishing your objective (*to get her to behave toward me as she used to*), you can change the action choice. Crucially important is that the source of changing your action is Nina and what she is saying and doing to you. You, as Treplev, should determine how you hear and receive Nina's "What's wrong with you?"

TREPLEV: And soon I'm going to kill myself in the same way.

Commentary: How does Nina hear these words from Treplev? Her lines below indicate that she does not know what's wrong with him. Does she believe him? Does it change her objective? At the end of his short monologue, he exits, and she does not follow him. This is significant. Perhaps she does not believe that he will actually kill himself.

Beat 8

Nina's Focus/Source: Treplev, specifically his strangeness.
Nina's Action: She might wish to get him to stop this behavior by confronting him: to make him feel on the spot.
Nina's How: Aggressively.

NINA: What is wrong with you? This isn't like you at all!

Beat 9

Treplev's Focus/Source: Nina's changed attitude.
Treplev's Action: To make her feel responsible.
Treplev's How: Aggressively (in response to Nina's how above).

TREPLEV: That's true! I began to change when you did. You've changed towards me and you know it. . . . You're cold to me, and my very presence bothers you.

Commentary: Even if the actor as Nina does not give you a changed attitude you can "see" the change in her. You can treat her as if she has changed toward you. When you accuse her of having changed, turning "cold" toward you, the implication is that there was a time when this was not the case. While you should exercise caution to never assume that what one character says about another character through dialogue is always true, with Treplev there is evidence to support the conclusion that Nina *has* changed toward him. Consider just how long it has been since she changed. For example, it is likely that these "changes" Treplev has been observing in Nina have not been going on for long, perhaps only since the arrival of Irina and, especially, Trigorin.

While Irina might very well prove a model for the kind of actor that Nina wants to be, Trigorin might prove more that just a model for a lover whom she wishes to have. Their arrival on the estate could have strong influences on Nina. Further, Treplev's "childish" behavior during the play-within-the-play in Act I could lead Nina to the conclusion that he is not someone with whom she wishes to continue a romantic relationship. During the imaginary time in between Act I and Act II, Treplev has witnessed Nina's withdrawal from him. If their relationship has changed, which is evident through the dialogue, presumably this imaginary period in between acts furthered that change.

Beat 10

Nina's Focus/Source: Treplev's odd behavior.
Nina's Action: To make him feel strange.
Nina's How: Critically.

NINA: You've been so irritable lately, and most of the time you talk in riddles, and I don't understand a word you're saying.

Commentary: Right in the middle of the line, Nina can shift her action or her how. Why would she do that? Because of the pressure that Trigorin might appear at any minute and the fact that she has still not succeeded in making Treplev leave. Also, as a reaction to Treplev's cryptic behavior, which she does not understand.

Beat 11

Nina's Focus/Source: The sea gull.
Nina's Action: Same as previous section.
Nina's How: Sarcastically.

NINA: (lines continue) And I suppose now that this sea gull, here, is some kind of symbol, too. Well,---

Commentary: In looking at Treplev's lines when he speaks next ("It all began the night my play failed . . ."), it appears he is not responding directly to the lines Nina is speaking now. The lines he speaks reveal what he actually listens to while Nina is speaking these lines above. It appears that Treplev was focused on something else when he responds below with: "It all began the night my play failed. Women never forgive failure." He did not respond by explaining what the dead sea gull symbolizes or by telling Nina that she is not simple minded. Right here, in the middle of Nina's lines, is an example of how an action can change while another character is speaking as shown in the next section.

> **Treplev's Focus/Source:** Nina seeing him as a failure.
> **Treplev's Action:** To make her feel cruel.
> **Treplev's How:** Resentfully.

NINA (lines continue):—forgive me, I don't understand that either . . .
   [*Putting the sea gull on the seat.*]

Commentary: Note that Nina has the activity of putting the sea gull on the seat. The actor playing Nina can do this while still maintaining the action and the how of it and allow the how of it to inform her movement in the way in which she places the sea gull on the bench.

NINA: (lines continue) I'm too simple minded to understand you.
TREPLEV: It all began the night my play failed. Women never forgive failure. Well, I burnt it! Every bit of it!

Commentary: In the section above, the actor playing Treplev may continue *to make Nina feel cruel*, although Nina may have changed from making him feel *on the spot* to *making him feel strange*. At some point, the actor playing Treplev may change his action as well. During his line "Well I burnt it!" he may choose *to make Nina feel shocked*. Such choices are always made because the previous action may not accomplish the objective. In analyzing the language, notice where Treplev changes the subject from his unhappiness to Nina. As the subject shifts, the action can shift, too.

> **Focus/Source:** Nina, and what she is concealing.
> **Action:** To make her feel sorry for him.
> **How:** Desperately.

TREPLEV (lines continue): *These lines are Treplev's* Oh, if you only knew how unhappy I am! And the way you've rejected me, I can't understand it! . . . It's as if I woke up one morning and found the lake suddenly drying up.

Focus/Source: Nina closing herself off to him.

Action: To make her feel wrong.

How: Aggressively.

TREPLEV (lines continue):   You said that you're too simple minded to understand me. Tell me, what's there to understand? Nobody liked my play, so now you despise my talent, and think I'm ordinary and insignificant, like all the rest of them . . . [*Stamping his foot.*]

Commentary: The stage directions indicate that Treplev stamps his foot after the last line. As Treplev, consider the following: What is the source of stamping your foot? Is it frustration in not getting what you want? Can you stamp your foot and use the stamping of the foot to continue to make Nina feel wrong in an aggressive way? Make the stamping of your foot drive the action into Nina, rather than simply sending your energy into the stage floor by stamping your foot, you send it into your acting partner. The stamping of the foot can be to jar the emotional life of the actor playing Nina. If you maintain the how of the action, to make her feel wrong *aggressively*, you can stamp your foot aggressively.

Beat 14

Treplev's Focus/Source: Nina still not giving you, as Treplev, what you want. Use this as a source for changing the action in order to continue to fight for your objective.

Treplev's Action: To make her feel sneaky.

Treplev's How: Poetically.

TREPLEV (lines continue): Oh, how well I understand. How well! It's like a nail in my head . . . Oh, damn it . . . And my pride . . . sucking my life blood . . . like a snake . . .

Transition: Trigorin enters.

Commentary: Treplev's next lines reveal that he has seen Trigorin enter. This may seem obvious, but keep in mind that you, as Treplev, have to actually see Trigorin enter. What does Trigorin's entrance mean to Treplev? Does he consider that Nina has been slyly waiting to see Trigorin? Does he consider that the two have planned a rendezvous? Does it trigger intense jealousy? If it triggers intense jealousy, rather than to try to "fake" the emotion of jealousy, try thinking about an action and the how of the action that would reveal jealousy, such as *to make Trigorin feel phony* with the how being *sarcastically*.

Treplev's Source/Focus: Trigorin, specifically that Nina has fallen in love with him.

Treplev's Action: To make him feel phony.

Treplev's How: Sarcastically.

TREPLEV: [*Sees Trigorin, who enters reading.*] But here comes the real genius, he walks like Hamlet himself, and with a book, too.

Commentary: Consider as Treplev where your focus should be placed. Although Trigorin's entrance is important, your objective is inextricably bound up in Nina, so keep Nina within your circle of attention. While you may focus on Trigorin for a moment, inevitably bring your focus back to Nina, refueled by Trigorin's entrance. Consider that the more you make Trigorin feel phony the more you indirectly affect Nina, reveal the pain that Treplev is dealing with, and forward your quest to achieve your objective. Though your focus on Trigorin is brief, make it count by fully committing to action.

Commentary: From Nina's point of view, you can assume that Trigorin enters in her sight range from Treplev's line, "The sun has hardly touched you and already you're smiling and your eyes are melting in its rays." Can you play an action on Treplev to show you have seen Trigorin? Can you play an action on Trigorin to let him know you have seen him? You can suspect that Trigorin wants to be alone with you, as you do him. When he sees you speaking with Treplev, you have to deal with the idea that Trigorin likely knows of Treplev's jealousy and knows that he cannot wait around in hopes that Treplev will leave. While none of this information is actually written in the play, it is in keeping with the play, and it is a valid use of the imagination in building circumstances that serve you as Nina and the play as a whole. Remember that playwrights for the most part give us just the dialogue. We have to fill in the rest of the story.

Nina's Focus/Source: Trigorin.

Nina's Action: To make Treplev feel unwanted.

Nina's How: Impatiently.

Commentary: Remember the Stakes, which suddenly increase. You may lose the opportunity to be alone with Trigorin.

Remember, too, the Obstacle, which now becomes Treplev arguing with you, as Nina. This is sure to keep Trigorin walking, rather than stopping to talk.

Treplev's Source/Focus: Decide to keep your focus on Trigorin or shift it back to Nina. Let's assume that you shift it back to Nina in order to read her reaction to Trigorin. Keep in mind that people see what they want to see and hear what they want to hear. What you see in looking at Nina can be her excitement that Trigorin has suddenly appeared.

Treplev's Action: To make her feel annoyed.

Treplev's How: Mockingly.

TREPLEV: [*Mimics.*] "Words, words, words."

Commentary: You, as Nina, should ask yourself how you hear Treplev's words. Consider how this moment affects your relationship with him. If you have chosen that you want to be alone with Trigorin, how does it affect you to have Treplev's present, arguing with you, and making you feel annoyed? (Stated action choice above.)

Treplev's Focus/Source: Nina. See her excitement about the arrival of Trigorin.

Treplev's Action: To make her feel disgusting.

Treplev's How: Condescendingly.

TREPLEV: . . . The sun has hardly touched you and already you're smiling and your eyes are melting in its rays. I won't bother you any more . . .

Commentary: The next piece of blocking has Treplev exiting to end the scene. Depending on how that blocking is structured, your focus may vary. If you are blocked to exit past Trigorin, you can play an action on him, perhaps making him feel threatened or insignificant or wrong. If you are to exit in the opposite direction, even as you turn your back and walk away, you can send action to either Trigorin or Nina. You can continue with the chosen action, (maybe *to make Nina feel disgusting*), and allow a new how (*quickly*), to inform the manner in which you walk off

TREPLEV: [*Goes out quickly.*]

Commentary: With the exit, the playwright has clearly signaled a transition. In the pre-performance work, ask yourself whether or not your character achieved the objective and how does this affect your next choice of objective?

Nina: What Do I Do If I Get or Don't Get What I Want?

Nina achieves her objective, which is *to get Treplev to leave*. At this point, she can turn to a new objective; one that serves her super-objective, such as *to get Trigorin to fall in love with me*. The dialogue does not specifically indicate what the scene is about; however, the events following it (their kiss, her covert message to him, their secret meeting, their affair, and her pregnancy) support the choice for that particular objective. More importantly, this objective could serve your super-objective, *to become a successful professional actress*, because Trigorin is a great writer who is from the theatre world of which you long to become a part. Being a successful playwright, Trigorin has connections and could help you to have the career you seek.

Treplev: What Do I Do If I Get or Don't Get What I Want?

Treplev does not achieve his objective, which is *to get Nina to behave towards me as she used to*. At this point, Treplev exits. He later attempts suicide. The next scene he appears in is with his mother, who is bandaging his head wound, a result of the suicide attempt. A strong possibility for an objective in the scene is *to get his mother to prevent the budding relationship between Nina and Trigorin*. It is in this way that you, as Treplev, can answer the question *What do I do if I get or don't get what I want?* at the end of this scene with Nina. He leaves Nina and Trigorin and considers and then attempts suicide, as a result of not getting what he wants, although the actual suicide attempt does not happen on stage.

Remembering It All: Marking Your Script

The work of analyzing the script, addressing the questions, and making choices takes time. As you make choices, you may want to write them down. When working with a script, simply write in the margin "guilty" or jot down, "loved/gently" to delineate that action choice for that particular section of the play. In the other margin, put your blocking such as "put sea gull on bench" and "XDL" (cross down left). There is no need to muddy up the script by writing out "make her feel guilty." As you will always be playing action, the word alone

Numbers in text refer to numbers in margin

S/F = Source/Focus

(I) = Irina

(T) = Trigorin

(S) = Shamrayev

(TP) = Treplev

Action and How of Action = Action/How of Action
Your blocking and activities can be in the opposite margin.

NINA, *alone.*[1] How strange it is to see a famous actress crying . . . and over nothing![2] And isn't it strange that a famous writer spends all his time fishing.[3] Here he is, a best seller, written about in all the papers, his pictures everywhere, his books translated into foreign languages, and . . . he gets all excited if he catches a couple of perch.[4] I always thought that famous people were proud and aloof and that they despised the crowd; I thought they used their glory and fame to get revenge on people who put wealth and position above everything else. But here they are crying, and fishing, and playing cards, and laughing and getting upset like everyone else.

TREPLEV *enters, carrying a gun and a dead sea gull.* Are you all alone?

NINA[5] Yes. TREPLEV *lays the sea gull at her feet.*[6] What does this mean?

TREPLEV I was rotten enough to kill this sea gull today. I lay it at your feet.

NINA[7] What's wrong with you?[8] *Picks up the sea gull and looks at it.*

TREPLEV, *after a pause.* And soon I'm going to kill myself in the same way.

NINA[9] What *is* wrong with you? This isn't like you at all

TREPLEV That's true! I began to change when you did. You've changed towards me and you know it. ... You're cold to me, and my very presence bothers you.

[10]NINA You've been so irritable lately, andmost of the time you talk in riddles and I don't understand a word you're saying. And [11]I suppose now that this sea gull, here, is some kind of symbol too.

Well, forgive me, I don't understand that either ... *Putting the sea gull on the seat.* I'm too simple-minded to understand you.

1. S/F → Image (I) DR
childish/disappointingly

2. S/F → Image (T) DL
childish/curiously

3. S/F → Image newspaper
page of (T) DR desire/
affectionately

4. S/F → Image of (I)
& (S) DC arguing (I)
petty/critically

5. S/F → (TP)
unwanted/rudely

6. S/F → Seagull
strange/disturbingly

7. S/F → (TP) strange/
tentatively

8. S/F → Seagull (TP)
wrong/gently

9. S/F → (TP)
on-the-spot/aggressively

10. S/F → (TP) strange/
critically

11. S/F → Seagull
strange/sarcastically

TREPLEV It all began the night my play failed. Women never forgive failure. Well, I burnt it! Oh, if you only knew how unhappy I am! And the way you've rejected me, I can't understand it! . . . It's as if I woke up one morning and found the lake suddenly drying up. You just said that you're too simple-minded to understand me. Tell me, what's there to understand? Nobody liked my play, so now you despire my talent, and think I'm ordinary and insigniicant, like all the rest of them . . . *Stamping his foot.* Oh, how well I understand. How well It's like a nail in my head . . . oh, damn it . . . And my pride . . . sucking my life blood . . . like a snake . . . Sees TRIGORIN, *who enters reading.* But here comes the real genius,[12] he walks like Hamlet himself, and with a book, too. *Mimics.* "Words, words, words." . . . The sun has hardly touched you, and already you're smiling and you eyes are melting in its rays. I won't bother you any more . . . *Goes out quickly.*

TRIGORIN, *making notes in his book.* Takes snuff and drinks vodka. Always wears black. A schoolmaster in love with her . . .

NINS Good morning, Boris Alexeyvich!

TRIGORIN Good morning. It seems that unexpectedly we're going to leave today. I don't suppose we'll meet again. I'm sorry. I don't often get a chance to meet young and interesting girls like you. I've forgotten what if feels like tobe eighteen or nineteen; in fact, I can't even imagine it any more. That's why the young girls in my novels and stories usually ring false. I wish I could change places with you, just for an hour, so I could know your thoughts and the kind of person you are.

NINA And I'd like to be in you place for a while.

TRIGORIN What for?

NINA So I'd know what it feels like to be a famous,to be a talented writer. What does it feel like to be famour? What does it do to you?

TRIGORIN What does it feel like? I don't know, I've never thought about it. *After a moment's thought.* It's one of two things, I suppose: either you exaggereate my fame, or it's nothing at all.

NINA But you must read about yourself in the papers?

TRIGORIN When they praise me I'm pleased, and when they attack me I'm in bad humor for a couple of days.

NINA What a wonderful world you live in! How I envy you—if only you knew! ... How different people's destinies are! Most people are all alike—unhappy. This obscure, tedious existence just drags on and on. And, then, there are others—like you, one in a million—who have a bright and interesting life, a life that has significance. Yours is a happy destiny.

TRIGORIN Mine! *Shrugs his shoulders.* You talk about fame and happiness, and his bright and interesting life I lead. But—to me will suffice. If you are on stage with more than one character, put a mark to indicate whom you are playing the action on. However, it is advised that you keep your script fairly clean as far as writing notes goes.

All of the work of analyzing a scene eventually finds expression through playing actions. To emphasize this, the notes you make in your script should be in the form of actions and the hows of those actions. There is no need to write out long sentences. The simpler you make the notations the better. If Treplev were in a scene with Nina, Masha, and Medvendenko and the action was on Masha, you, as Treplev, can jot "Ma-unwanted." The sooner you can memorize your lines, and the blocking and action choices, the sooner you can leave the script off-stage when rehearsing. The following example is give of how you might mark your script in a simple, but effective way.

Prepartion And Rehearsal

Let's say you are playing Treplev and are in your first rehearsal with the actor playing Nina. You will have done your homework beforehand in addressing the questions *Who am I? Where am I? When am I there?*, and *What do I want?* You may find one of two things once you start rehearsing. One is that is your objectives and action choices work brilliantly, and you can look forward to many smooth and happy rehearsals, working on defining the action and the how of the action. Another possibility is that at least some of the objective or action choices you have chosen don't seem to work as well as you would like.

If the objective you've chosen is *to make Nina turn her back on Trigorin*, you may find that the objective is too vague, doesn't really inspire you toward action, or perhaps you have no clear sense of what it would really look like for Nina to turn her back on Trigorin, unless she physically turns her body, which is more of a blocking choice than a response to your objective. In that case, change the objective. There is no harm in discovering that the objective doesn't seem to work. In large part that is what early rehearsals can be about, discovering if objectives work and discovering action choices.

Once you've set an objective, pick a first action, such as *to make Nina feel guilty*. One possibility is that your action seems to work for you. You may choose *to make Nina feel loved* and find that choice of action feels connected and in service to the play. Or perhaps you find that the action doesn't seem to work for the scene. Perhaps it is not strong enough, or it is too strong, or it seems unfocused, or it doesn't feel natural. If you, as Treplev, mark in your script *to make Nina feel loved* for your first action, you may discover within the first 30 seconds of rehearsal that a better choice is *to make her feel guilty*. Again, there is no harm done. It is the exploratory nature of rehearsal to find these things out.

Even an action that serves you well at the start of the scene may undergo change as the scene progresses. At some point you will change the action if it is not helping you accomplish the objective, or you might change the how of the action, such as from *nobly* to *sarcastically*. However, avoid making these changes in your head at home—try, instead, to discover them in the rehearsal process. Make your objective choice and your first action choice, and then get in there and play. At some point, by fully giving yourself over to playing action, you may find yourself intuitively doing something interesting. You may feel, "Wow, that worked well. I wonder what I did in the heat of the moment that seemed to feel right?" At that point, capture on your script (or with a mental note) what you were doing that seemed to be working so well in terms of action. It is frustrating to take a break and go back to a scene and find the thread of what you were doing earlier has been lost. You might be tempted to imitate what you thought you were doing, but this imitation will lack spontaneity.

If you have given specific thought (and made a note in the script) as to what was working as action, you will have an anchor to where your own intuition led you in the heat of the moment, and you can maintain spontaneity through playing an action. Because your action is not an imitation, it is something you can repeat night after night, with freshness and natural differences as you work towards making someone else feel an emotion.

More Examples of Applying the Methodology

THIS CHAPTER OFFERS MORE EXAMPLES OF HOW TO apply the methodology. It is not necessary to analyse an entire play in order to exercise aspects of the approach for your own practice and development. The examples that follow include monologues, poetry, lines from texts and lines that you author yourself.

In preparing monologues for auditions and during rehearsals for plays, use images of the other characters and things around you. Using images that help trigger feelings in you appropriate to the *Who am I?* is the best way to create dynamic work. There are differences between working on a monologue for audition and practice purposes versus for a play in which you have been cast. As an example, in working on a Juliet monologue or soliloquy for an audition, you have the opportunity create and use the image of an attractive Romeo of your own choosing. Cast in a play, you would find something attractive and focus on an aspect or image of the Romeo cast opposite you.

It is not the intent of these practice selections to offer "correct" interpretations from a critical perspective. There are other possible interpretations of the material, and other choices for objectives, images, action choices, and ways of playing the action. As you address each monologue, begin to answer the larger questions of *Who am I?, Where am I?, and When am I there?* Gradually narrow to address the monologue by defining the where, when, what, and how of your character as revealed through the specific lines, as well as by choosing and specifically defining sources/images, action changes, and other elements that are relevant. The examples below offer beginning suggestions in addressing the questions. In-depth analyses would provide much richer and detailed insights for playing the roles.

Yelena in *Uncle Vanya* by Anton Chekhov

YELENA: [*Alone*] There is nothing worse than to know the secret of another human being, and to realize there's nothing you can do to help them. [*In deep thought.*] Obviously he is not in love with her, but why shouldn't he marry her? To be sure, she is not beautiful, yet she is good and kind, pure of heart, and so sensible that she would make an excellent wife for a country doctor of his age. [*Pause.*] I can understand the poor child's feelings. Here she lives in the midst of this desperate loneliness with no one about her except those gray shadows that pass for human beings, who do nothing but eat, drink, and talk trivial commonplaces. And, then, who from time to time should appear upon the scene among them but this Dr. Astrov, so unlike the rest—so handsome, interesting, fascinating . . . It is like seeing the moon rising, rich and full, in the darkness. Oh, to be able to surrender yourself—and forget oneself—body and soul to such a man! Yes, I too, am a little in love with him! Yes, without him I am lonely; when I think of him, I smile. Uncle Vanya says I have mermaid's blood in my veins: "For once in your life, let yourself go!" Perhaps I should. Oh, to be free as a bird, to fly away from all those drowsy faces and their monotonous mumblings and forget that they have existed at all! Oh, to forget oneself and what one is . . . But I am a coward; I am afraid; and tortured by my conscience. He comes here every day now. I can guess why, and already my guilt condemns me. I should like to fall on my knees at Sonia's feet and beg her to forgive me and weep . . . but . . .

Commentary

Images can help to generate experience. If you have been cast in a play, use images of the actors cast in the play with you. If it is for an audition, you can conceive images of characters or borrow images of actual people, such as from paintings and photographs that help you to connect to Yelena's experience. It is important that your images be specific and detailed. They should help put you into the experience the character is going through. Put images in different places. For example, try an image of Astrov about ten feet in front of and five feet above you out toward the audience. This will help to bring your voice and focus forward and out, which will help the audience to experience the execution of your choices through your release of action onto the image. It takes time to simply stand, breathe, and use your imagination to create or recall (if you originally used photos and/or paintings) images that are clear and that effectively engage you. The more you do it, the easier and better you will get at it. Remember, too, that you are rehearsing your body, as well as your mind and imagination, and there may be discomfort initially. You may resist remaining still and imagining an image four feet out in front of you. It may take time to begin to feel grounded; to really see the image and allow yourself to be affected by it. Your imagination will get stronger through use and, through repetition, your body will begin to get used to this way of working. It will become easier and easier over time.

Although the work of creating or recalling the images, choosing actions and the hows of the actions and practicing the monologue with these choices may seem very mechanical initially, through rehearsal your work can grow more spontaneous until you are no longer thinking about the images, actions or anything else, but living totally in the moment.

Reading One: Understanding the Story

Read the play through once for the overall story, the experiences and the impressions it leaves with you. Briefly, in *Uncle Vanya*, important elements of the story include inertia and longing for love but not taking action consistent with obtaining the love desired. An older man, Professor Serebryakov, and his young second wife, Yelena, have arrived on his estate. He inherited the estate through his first wife, who passed away. Yelena is restless and has fallen in love with Doctor Astrov. Her stepdaughter Sonya is of about the same age as she is. Sonya, too, is in love with the doctor, though he is not responsive to her. Sonya has asked Yelena to find out how he feels about her.

Reading Two: Gathering the Facts

The facts provide a foundation from which you can make strong choices that serve the character, the play, and the theme of the play. The following facts are pertinent to the monologue, though there are many others that can be observed through a careful reading of the play. Yelena was born and went to school in St. Petersburg. Yelena's husband, Serebryakov, is much older than she is. He is a retired professor. He often yells at and criticizes her. Yelena finds the doctor handsome and attractive. Just prior to the monologue, Yelena had a talk with Sonya, in which Sonya revealed that she has been in love with Astrov for six years and that she does not know how Astrov feels about her. Sonya is Serebryakov's daughter through his deceased first wife, Vanya's sister. Yelena offers to talk to Astrov to find out whether or not Astrov loves Sonya. Serebryakov wants to sell the estate, which would leave Vanya and Vanya's mother homeless.

The monologue takes place on an afternoon in September on Serebryakov's estate in the country. Serebryakov and Yelena are visiting.

Reading Three: Yelena's Point of View

Yelena is unhappily married to an older man, retired Professor Serebryakov. He suffers from various ailments, and it is likely that there is little or no romance in their lives. Yelena, who is much younger, longs for romance, love, and a meaningful existence. With Serebryakov, she has none of it. Doctor Astrov is not only handsome and dashing, he is someone who would make a good husband; someone with whom she can feel connected to something meaningful: helping him to help others. His love of beauty finds fulfillment in her, which makes her feel beautiful. His attention makes her feel alive. In addition to the fact that she has a husband, her dilemma is Sonya, with whom she would like to develop a loving, caring relationship. Sonya, though close in age, is her stepdaughter. Yelena is torn between her desire to help Sonya and her desire as a woman who seeks fulfillment. This leaves her vulnerable to Astrov. However, her self-characterization as a "coward" finds expression in numerous ways, including resisting Astrov's advances, despite an inner passion to be with him.

Who am I?

Passions: I dislike the dull, meaningless people around the estate, such as Vanya and Waffles, an impoverished landowner. I dislike myself, my husband, and my life. I love Sonya and am in love with Astrov. I hate not having a meaningful purpose in life.

Body Age: I am in my late twenties.

Relationships: I am the wife of Serebryakov and the stepmother to Sonya.

Ask the question, *Who are you?* (as well as *Who am I?*), referring to the other characters in the play. In the monologue, Yelena refers to other characters. Identifying who the other characters are to Yelena will help you to see who she is when she is with them. This will affect the choices you make. For example, ask: *Who am I (Yelena) when I am with Astrov? with Sonya? with my husband? with Vanya? with Waffles?*

Where am I and When am I there?

I am in the drawing room of my husband's country estate in summer. It is afternoon, several weeks after arriving. I am alone, awaiting the arrival of Astrov, the man I have fallen in love with.

Yelena is removed from city life and things that help distract her from herself. During the time that has passed at the estate, a mutual attraction has developed between Astrov and Yelena. Astrov is soon to arrive to meet with her and show her his maps. She has just finished speaking with Sonya and has agreed to find out if Astrov has romantic feelings for Sonya. The soliloquy takes place immediately after Sonya's exit, as Yelena waits for Astrov's arrival. Yelena is interrupted by Astrov's entrance.

What do I want? (super-objective):

To find a meaningful purpose in life.

What do I want? (objective for this monologue):

To get Astrov to reveal his romantic feelings.

What/who are the obstacles? This meeting could end badly. I don't know if I can control my own feelings. I have a husband and my stepdaughter is also in love with Astrov. My own cowardice and fear are in the way.

What is at stake? It could prove disastrous to the family if I were to have an affair with Astrov.

Transition: Sonya exits, leaving Yelena alone on stage.

Beat 1

Source: Image of Sonya, seated in a chair down left, crying.
Action: To make her feel cared for.
How: Gently.

YELENA: There is nothing worse than to know the secret of another human being, and to realize there's nothing you can do to help them. [*In deep thought.*]

Beat 2

Source: Image of Astrov, standing down center looking at Sonya seated down left.

Action: To make Astrov feel mysterious.

How: Curiously.

SONYA: Obviously he is not in love with her, but why shouldn't he marry her?

Beat 3

Source: Image of Sonya working, sitting, down left.

Action: To make Sonya feel deserving.

How: Approvingly.

ASTROV: To be sure, she is not beautiful, yet she is good and kind, pure of heart, and so sensible that she would make an excellent wife for a country doctor of his age. [*Pause.*]

Beat 4

Source: Image of Waffles and Vanya seated at a table, engaged in meaningless talk. The image can be out over the heads of the audience a few rows from down stage.

Action: To make Vanya feel silly.

How: Chidingly.

WAFFLES: I can understand the poor child's feelings. Here she lives in the midst of this desperate loneliness with no one about her except those gray shadows who pass for human beings, who do nothing but eat, drink, and talk trivial commonplaces.

Beat 5

Source: Image of Astrov arriving, just to the right of the image of Waffles and Vanya.

Action: To make him feel attractive.

How: Coyly.

YELENA: And, then, who from time to time should appear upon the scene among them but this Dr. Astrov, so unlike the rest—so handsome, interesting, fascinating . . .

Beat 6

Source: Image of Astrov, still to the right of previous image, but on a moonlit summer night in a garden.

Action: To make Astrov feel alluring.
How: Maintain coyly.

YELENA: It is like seeing the moon rising, rich and full, in the darkness.

Beat 7

Source: Image of Astrov and Yelena alone in the garden, down right.
Action: To make him feel encouraged.
How: Seductively.

YELENA: Oh, to be able to surrender yourself—and forget oneself—body and soul to such a man!

Beat 8

Source: Image of herself looking at Astrov walking away from down right, toward off left.
Action: To make herself feel encouraged.
How: Teasingly.

YELENA: Yes, I, too, am a little in love with him! Yes, without him I am lonely; when I think of him, I smile.

Beat 9

Source: Image of herself as a beautiful mermaid over the heads of the audience left.
Action: To make herself feel beautiful.
How: Encouragingly.

YELENA: Uncle Vanya says I have mermaid's blood in my veins: "For once in your life, let yourself go!"

Beat 10

Source: Image of herself being abused by Serebryakov in the same place.
Action: To make herself feel encouraged.
How: Daringly

YELENA: Perhaps I should.

Beat 11

Source: Image of herself being kissed by Astrov in the garden, on stage, down right.

Action: To make herself feel inspired.
How: Rebelliously.

YELENA: Oh, to be free as a bird, to fly away from all those drowsy faces and their monotonous mumblings and forget that they have existed at all! Oh, to forget oneself and what one is . . .

Beat 12

Source: Same place as previous image, but Yelena pulling back from the kiss.
Action: To make herself feel ashamed.
How: Dispiritedly.

YELENA: But I am a coward; I am afraid; and tortured by my conscience.

Beat 13

Source: Image of Astrov smiling at Yelena, same place.
Action: To make him feel dangerous.
How: Fearfully.

YELENA: He comes here every day now. I can guess why, and already my guilt condemns me.

Beat 14

Source: Image of Sonya longing for Astrov, on stage in chair left.
Action: To make Sonya feel loved.
How: Submissively.

ASTROV: I should like to fall on my knees at Sonia's feet and beg her to forgive me and weep . . . but . . .

Transition: Astrov enters the room.

Commentary

Chekhov has Astrov enter just as Yelena returns to talking about Sonya. Sonya has asked Yelena to speak to Astrov on her behalf. Yelena's last line refers directly to Sonya and Yelena's desire for forgiveness. She says "my guilt condemns me" just as Astrov walks into the room, not at the point in the monologue where she is talking about letting herself go. Therefore, her state of being when Astrov enters is primarily one of guilt and shame. This does not mean the excitement and passion are not part of her. It means that she feels guilty about her excitement. Remember, too, Yelena's *Who am I?*

changes depending on who she is with. As Yelena, ask yourself, *Who am I?* when I am with Sonya and how does that change when I am with Astrov?

Emilia in *Othello* by William Shakespeare

EMILIA: But I do think it is their husband's faults
If wives do fall. Say that they slack their duties,
And pour our treasures into foreign laps,
Or else break out in peevish jealousies,
Throwing restraint upon us; or say they strike us,
Or scant our former having in despite;
Why, we have gauls, and though we have some grace,
Yet we have some revenge. Let husbands know
Their wives have sense like them: they see and smell
And have their palates both for sweet and sour,
As husbands have. What is it they do
When they change us for others? Is it sport?
I think it is: and doth affection breed it?
I think it doth: is't frailty that thus errs?
It is so, too: and have we not affections?
Desires for sport, and frailty, as men have?
Then let them use us well: else let them know,
The ills we do, their ills instruct us so.

Reading One: Understanding the Play

Othello is about status, power, prejudice, and deception. It is about jealousy, violence, and love. Othello, a general in the army of Venice, is led to believe his wife Desdemona has been unfaithful through a rumor started by Iago, his ensign, for Iago's own purposes. The play ends violently. (If you were cast in the play, your examination of the play would be much deeper and more detailed. For the purpose of examining this monologue, these "bare bones" details will suffice.)

Reading Two: Gathering the Facts

The facts provide a foundation from which you can make strong choices that serve the character, the play, and the theme of the play. The following facts are pertinent to the monologue; however, many others can be observed through a careful reading of the play.

Emilia is Desdemona's attendant.

Desdemona is married to Othello, who is a general and the governor of Cyprus.

Emilia's husband is Iago, an ensign under Othello.

Iago is abusive towards Emilia.

Othello has recently been angry and jealous over Desdemona, believing that she is committing adultery.

Desdemona is innocent, and neither she nor Emilia understand Othello's behavior.

Desdemona has been ordered to bed by Othello. He will join her shortly.

Othello has told Desdemona to dismiss Emilia.

In a state of confusion, Desdemona asks Emilia if there are such women who would commit adultery, as this relates directly to Othello's inferences.

Reading Three: Emilia's Point of View

At first, Emilia helps her husband in his effort to get ahead by stealing a handkerchief from Desdemona. She later regrets her action, defends her lady's honor, and confesses her part in the trick. Emilia thinks there are many women who would commit adultery and defends their actions in the monologue.

This is not a soliloquy, as it is spoken to Desdemona. If you are preparing for the scene in rehearsal, and you are working alone, use images of the actor playing Desdemona. This will help you to connect with the other actor when you rehearse and perform. While you, as Emelia, can have an image of Othello, you can simultaneously play an action on Desdemona, such as to make her feel inspired. The image you pick of Othello should affect you. For example, imagine Othello putting you down in some way. This method is not meant to replace your other work with classical texts, such as scanning, phrasing, and other approaches to clarifying, elucidating, and speaking Shakespeare's language; it is meant to be applied in combination with it.

Who am I?

Passions: I dislike the freedom men have to cheat while women must remain loyal. I hate that men cheat on and abuse women. I am jealous of the freedom that men have to do what they want.

Body Age: Adult, but no specific age is given in the play.

Relationships: I am the wife of Iago, who is Othello's ensign. I am Desdemona's attendant, but also her closest friend

Status: As Desdemona's attendant I am of lower status, but we are good friends, and there is a degree of intimacy between us that levels our interaction in private. My husband is an ensign, of lower rank (status) than Desdemona's husband, General Othello. My status below Desdemona parallels Iago's status below Othello.

Who am I? in terms of Who are you? Who am I? when I am with Desdemona? Othello? Iago? Remember that the Who am I? shifts, depending on the person you are with.

Where am I and When am I there?

I am in Venice, Italy, in Othello and Desdemona's bedchamber. It is evening, soon after Othello struck Desdemona and sent her to the bedchamber.

Othello will be returning shortly to "deal" with Desdemona. As neither Desdemona nor Emilia know when he will return, the fact that he may return at any moment ups the stakes to say what needs to be said.

What do I want?

To get Desdemona to stand up to Othello.

Remember, you create what it is you want on behalf of the character based on a combination of the given circumstances, logical thinking, and your imagination. The objective *to get Desdemona to stand up to Othello* is offered as an example, but it is not the only possibility for the monologue.

How do I get it?

Although Desdemona is of higher status than Emilia, the two are intimate friends. Emilia has been abused by her husband and, therefore, recognizes similar behavior in Othello. This can be reflected in the way in which she plays actions. Resentment toward her husband also can be reflected in the way in which she plays an action. For example, you, as Emilia can make Desdemona feel wrong, *resentfully*.

What/who are the obstacles? Desdemona's love of Othello, her views on marriage and her role as wife.

What is at stake? My honor and dignity.

Beat 1

Source/Focus: Image of Iago, Emilia's husband, cheating on her.
Action: To make Desdemona feel wrong.
How: Respectfully.

OTHELLO: But I do think it is their husbands' faults
If wives do fall.

Beat 2

> **Source/Focus:** Desdemona's naiveté.
> **Action:** Continue to make Desdemona feel wrong.
> **How:** Maintain respectfully.

OTHELLO: Say that they slack their duties,
And pour our treasures into foreign laps,

Beat 3

> **Source/Focus:** Image of Othello slapping Desdemona.
> **Action:** To make Desdemona feel belittled.
> **How:** Resentfully.

OTHELLO: Or else break out in peevish jealousies,
Throwing restraint upon us; or say they strike us,
Or scant our former having in despite;

Beat 4

> **Source/Focus:** Desdemona's fear.
> **Action:** To make Desdemona feel challenged.
> **How:** Conspiratorially.

OTHELLO: Why, we have gauls, and though we have some grace,
Yet we have some revenge.

Beat 5

> **Source/Focus:** Image of Othello.
> **Action:** To make Desdemona feel inspired.
> **How:** Belligerently.

OTHELLO: Let husbands know
Their wives have sense like them: they see and smell
And have their palates both for sweet and sour,
As husbands have.

Commentary

While you, as Emilia, can have an image of Othello, you can simultaneously play the action of making Desdemona feel inspired. The image you pick of Othello should affect you in some way. For example,
imagine Othello insulting you.

Beat 6

> **Source/Focus:** Image of Iago.
> **Action:** To make Iago feel pathetic.
> **How:** Indignantly.

EMILIA: What is it they do
When they change us for others? Is it sport?
I think it is: and doth affection breed it?
I think it doth: is't frailty that thus errs?
It is so, too:

Beat 7

> **Source/Focus:** Desdemona's childishness.
> **Action:** To make Desdemona feel included.
> **How:** Lovingly.

EMILIA: and have we not affections?
Desires for sport, and frailty, as men have?

Beat 8

> **Source/Focus:** Image of Othello.
> **Action:** To make him feel threatened.
> **How:** Stoically.

EMILIA: Then let them use us well: else let them know,
The ills we do, their ills instruct us so.

Male or Female in *Sonnet Number One* by William Shakespeare

A sonnet can be a useful tool for working alone, exercising the imagination, and playing actions and releasing the actions in different ways. As there is no play to analyze, use your imagination fully in addressing the questions *Who am I?, Where am I?, When am I there?, What do I want?,* and creating action choices, as well as how you will play them. The sonnet can help give you information for addressing the questions, but you can invent your own answers. You might repeat a given beat a half dozen times, clarifying the image, releasing the action and playing with it in different ways through varying the how of it. Once specific images and actions have been chosen, it is important to pracitice seeing the images, allowing yourself to be affected by them, and releasing actions onto them until it becomes second nature to do so.

Use the exercise to warm your voice and organize your breathing. Add gestures to get your body involved, connecting the gestures to the actions and the hows of the actions. Once the work of specifying action choices is done, and you have exercised releasing them onto the image, work on the rhythm and pace of the release. For the exercise, there is no need to do research on the sonnet in terms of what Shakespeare may have meant, who it may have actually been written for, and other historical details. For this exercise, treat it as if the only information you have about this sonnet is the lines themselves.

SONNET 1:   From fairest creatures we desire increase,
That thereby beauties rose might never die,
But as the riper should by time decrease
His tender heir might bear his memory.
But thou, contracted to thine own bright eyes,
Feed'st thy light's flame with self-substantial fuel,
Making a famine where abundance lies,
Thyself thy foe, to thy sweet self too cruel.
Thou that art now the world's fresh ornament
And only herald to the gaudy spring,
Within thine own bud buriest thy content,
And, tender churl, mak'st waste in niggarding.
Pity the world, or else this glutton be,
To eat the world's due, by the grave and thee.

The first part of the work on Shakespeare's sonnets and plays should be to analyze the text in order to determine what you are specifically saying. Bear in mind that about 98 percent of the words Shakespeare used are in use today. There may be some words that you might not understand, but there are tools you can use, such as *Shakespeare's Words; a Glossary & Language Companion* by David Crystal and Ben Crystal. You can also paraphrase the lines in order to help you to better understand the original text. Assuming you have a clear and specific understanding of what it is that you are saying, you can turn to addressing the questions *Who am I?, Where am I?, When am I there?,* and *What do I want?* through your imagination, thereby creating a world for yourself to work within. Taking liberties with the sonnet, you can create your own circumstances for the sake of exercising the imagination and releasing actions. For example:

Who am I?

A man (can be reversed and modified for a woman).

Passions: I like romantic evenings. I hate growing old without leaving behind children. I hate being alone and I wish to have a family. I love children. I love poetry and words. I love my wife, Helen, but hate her unwillingness to have children.

Age: 30

Relationships: I have a wife, Helen, and two strong families, who want us to have children.

Status: I am poet who has some family money and, therefore, enough to support a family of my own.

Where am I and When am I there?

I am in our bedroom, alone with her, in a small, but comfortable, warm house, in a town with houses inhabited by couples with children. It is "present day" to the time this sonnet was written. It is after the first six months of marriage without intimacy, at dusk on a cold winter's evening, during the usual time that we prepare for bed.

What do I want?

To get her to submit herself to me in an enthusiastic way.

What/who are the obstacles? My wife fears the pain of childbirth and fears it may detract from her looks, as she has seen her friends became less attractive, worn out, and older looking through raising a family. Her body is rigid.

Stakes: We might remain childless. Our families and friends will look down on us. There will be no one to care for us in our old age, no legacy, no grandchildren.

Commentary: Try to make the person attractive to you. This can include her looks, her personality, and something special about her that connects with you. Make her someone you could be very much in love with and who you want to be the mother of your children. Find ways to make this imagination work pleasurable and easy for yourself. Let your imagination go, picturing her in a nightgown, the room, a fireplace, hear snow falling on the roof, the distant sound of a neighbor's new-born baby crying for milk. Picture the intimacy of the scene. Imagine her name, her age, her height, hair color, shape, disposition, and attitude.

For the exercise, imagine that you are standing near the fireplace; you can see the fire reflected in her eyes. Make her someone who you are totally devoted to. See also, in her face, the obstacle to your getting her to submit to you; perhaps see it in the way that she holds tension in the brow. You can also imbue her with fear; for example, fear about childbirth. But then see what her face would look like if she agreed to your objective; that she felt relieved or at least willing to try. Then put the obstacle back in her face and begin the sonnet, using the sonnet to help you to get what you want, but using it specifically with action choices.

Beat 1

The entire piece can be practiced with her, as an image, standing before you. See her alive and three-dimensional, not as a picture. Further, see in her the suggestions below in "Source/Focus."

> **Source/Focus:** Her resistance.
> **Action:** To make her feel beautiful.
> **How:** Admiringly.

MAN:　From fairest creatures we desire increase,
That thereby beauties rose might never die,

Beat 2

> **Source/Focus:** Her fear of growing old.
> **Action:** To make her feel relieved.
> **How:** Authoritatively.

MAN:　But as the riper should by time decrease
his tender heir might bear his memory.

Beat 3

> **Source/Focus:** Her stubbornness.
> **Action:** To make her feel fear.
> **How:** Condescendingly.

MAN:　But thou, contracted to thine own bright eyes,
Feed'st thy light's flame with self-substantial fuel,
Making a famine where abundance lies,
Thyself thy foe, to thy sweet self too cruel.

Beat 4

> **Source/Focus:** Her selfishness.

Action: To make her feel vain.
How: Warily.

MAN: Thou that art now the world's fresh ornament
And only herald to the gaudy spring,
Within thine own bud buriest thy content,
And, tender churl, mak'st waste in niggarding.

Beat 5

Source/Focus: Her shame.
Action: To make her feel challenged.
How: Prophetically.

MAN: Pity the world, or else this glutton be,
To eat the world's due, by the grave and thee.

Action on an Audience

As was mentioned in Chapter 4, there are times when the aesthetics of the writing dictates or a directorial choice is made: that a play be staged without a "fourth wall", the imaginary division between the audience and the actors. In this dynamic, you, as the *Who am I?* may be required to speak directly to the audience. For example, Richard III has a long soliloquy at the beginning of William Shakespeare's *Richard III*.

RICHARD III: Now is the winter of our discontent
Made glorious summer by this sun of York,
And all the clouds that lour'd upon our house
In the deep bosom of the ocean buried.
Now are our brows bound with victorious wreaths,
Our bruised arms hung up for monuments,
Our stern alarums changed to merry meetings,
Our dreadful marches to delightful measures.
Grim-visaged War hath smoothed his wrinkled front,
And now, instead of mounting barbed steeds
To fright the souls of fearful adversaries,
He capers nimbly in a lady's chamber
To the lascivious pleasing of a lute.
But I, that am not shaped for sportive tricks
Nor made to court an amorous looking-glass,
I, that am rudely stamped and want love's majesty
To strut before a wanton ambling nymph,

I, that am curtailed of this fair proportion,
Cheated of feature by dissembling nature,
Deformed, unfinished, sent before my time
Into this breathing world scarce half made up,
And that so lamely and unfashionable
That dogs bark at me as I halt by them,
Why, I, in this weak piping time of peace
Have no delight to pass away the time
Unless to spy my shadow in the sun
And descant on my own deformity.

If the choice has been made that you, as Richard III, should speak to the audience, then this must be taken into account in your approach. One way to do this is by speaking to *individual* audience members. In so doing, the other audience members will feel included. However, you should shift your focus from one member to another or or to an image, as the subject matter of the text changes or you recognize that the text shifts in some way. You should always play action on the audience members, as well. For example, below is how several of the lines might be played:

Beat

> **Source/Focus:** Audience member
> **Action:** To make her feel sorry for me
> **How:** Gently

RICHARD III: But I, that am not shaped for sportive tricks
Nor made to court an amorous looking-glass,

Beat

> **Source/Focus:** Image of self on back wall of theatre
> **Action:** To make self feel ugly
> **How:** Shamefully

RICHARD III: I, that am rudely stamped and want love's majesty
To strut before a wanton ambling nymph,

Beat

> **Source/Focus:** Another audience member
> Action: To make him feel sympathetic.
> How: Indignantly

RICHARD III: I, that am curtailed of this fair proportion,

Cheated of feature by dissembling nature,
Deformed, unfinished, sent before my time
Into this breathing world scarce half made up,

Beat
> **Source/Focus:** Another audience member.
> **Action:** To make her feel uncomfortable
> **How:** Aggressively

RICHARD III: And that so lamely and unfashionable
That dogs bark at me as I halt by them,

While direct address to the audience is best done by focusing on one audience member at a time, images can also be incorporated into your work. In this way, your focus can shift from an audience member, to an image, to another audience member, and so forth. Choose a specific objective for each soliloquy, which can be articulated in terms of what you want to get the audience to do, such as *to reassure you that you are justified in taking necessary action to achieve your desires.*

Male or Female Using Lines from *Savage/Love* by Sam Shepard and Joseph Chaikin

In a more simplified way to practice, you can use lines from certain plays, such as Sam Shepard and Joseph Chaikin's, *Savage/Love*, without addressing the questions, *Who am I?, Where am I* and *When am I there?*, and *What do I want?* In this way you are free to invent objectives and/or to play actions and the hows of the actions.

MALE OR FEMALE: You
Who make me believe that we're lovers
You
Who let me pretend
You
Who reminds me of myself
You
Who control me

By taking small sections of text such as the above, you can practice with a friend, choosing actions and releasing them onto one another. You can also work alone using images and objects.

In working with a friend you can delineate one of you as "A" and the other as "B".

A: You
Who make me believe that we're lovers.
B: You
Who let me pretend
A: You
Who remind me of myself
B: You
Who control me

Sample Exercise 1: Actions with Objectives

A and B choose objectives for the exercise. For example, A chooses: *to get B to stop lying* and B chooses: *to get A to stop trying to control every facet of the relationship*. A chooses a first action, such as *to make B feel wrong*. B allows the action to affect him/her. A and B repeat this exchange several times. B notices how s/he feels and how s/he intuitively wants to respond. B takes this observation and articulates it in terms of an action, such as *to make A feel responsible for their problems*, and then plays that action on A.

Armed with one action each, A repeats the first line and action and B responds with his/her first line and action, and so on.

Sample Exercise 2: Actions and the Hows of the Actions Without Objectives.

A and B read the lines several times. A chooses a first action and B chooses a first action. They then play the lines with these first action choices committing themselves to affecting each other, and noticing their impulses to change the actions or the how's of the actions at some point. For example, as a first action, A chooses *to make B feel sneaky in an accusing way* and B chooses *to make A feel shallow in an intimidating way*. Both actors experiment with allowing the other person to affect them in such a way that the how of the action begins to change. For example, A may change from making B feel sneaky in an accusing way to a sarcastic way, and so on.

Sample Exercise 3: Solo Work

Working alone, select a different action and image per line. Practice seeing the images in different places. Practice releasing the actions onto the images. Build speed into the exercise. Learn to see an image quickly, release the action quickly and then move onto the next image and action.

You can also practice soliloquies and lines of text on your own using direct address. For example, you can imagine an audience before you and use single lines from *Savage/Love* playing actions on imagined individual audience members. Imagining a live audience before you, allowing yourself to simply stand before it and take it in can be a very good way to prepare yourself for performance. Taken further, using your imagination, see specific audience members at various places throughout, and release action choices onto them.

Creating Your Own Text

To increase your skill and comfort in using this method, you can practice when you are alone by writing your own lines of text and using them in for playing actions on images in an infinite variety of ways. For example, the line "Where have you been?" can be applied, independent of any specific context, to an image of your romantic partner who comes home late. The source and focus can be this partner or spouse and the fact that he is late. The objective can be *to get him/r to tell you what/he has been doing*. The action can be *to make him feel on the spot*, and the how can be *confrontationally*.

There are many possible ways to practice using the approach, although working with soliloquies, monologues and dialogue from plays and poetry is best. You can combine sonnet exercises with voice and movement work, so the voice and movement exercises are not done in isolation from text, but connected to imagination, objective, action, and the how of the action through the lines. For example, use your voice and/or body to send action in different ways. You can play with the how of the action through using your voice in different ways, such as *seductively, sarcastically, righteously*, or *sweetly*. In the same way, you can connect movement to the how of the action: move *aggressively, tentatively, gingerly*, or *drunkenly*. Initially, pay attention to yourself in order to get specific, refined, and exacting in your choice of the how. By doing such work repeatedly you will get comfortable with a specific how of voice or movement as it becomes second nature, and you can eventually take your focus off of yourself and put it on the other character, image, or thing that is the object of your action release.

Conclusion

READING ABOUT ACTING IS NOT AS EXCITING AS DOING
it, but it is through experimentation and thoughtful application of
new methods that we grow as actors. Most actors count themselves
lucky to be able to do something they love, and finding ways to hone
and improve acting techniques will keep your work fresh and alive.
Use this book and its powerful principles in approaching a role. Each
principle works in concert, serving and helping one another. Through
the work you will develop a strong sense of your ability to use imagination to create character and given circumstances consistent with
the play. Once you firmly grasp the intellectual outlines of those given
circumstances, remind yourself of the importance of vulnerability,
and practice taking in those imaginary circumstances through the
senses of the *Who am I?*

While some in an audience may have the idea the acting is an
"either you have it or you don't have it" gift, equally as many think a
"good" actor must endure anguish and suffering for the art. The truth
lies somewhere in between. It takes mindful effort to apply the methodology. However, that does not mean your work need be a tedious
chore. Children typically don't suffer when playing make-believe. Seek
to be like a child at play in performing a role. Maintain a sense of
curiosity and imagination to help you engender joy in acting. If the
process looks like drudgery, look to how you can inject a personally
beneficial tone into the work. Look for the opportunities to exercise
and strengthen your imagination. Look for the opportunities to play.

In your work, seek to apply the specific questioning techniques
and habits of script notation when you prepare for a role, and, at the
same time, remember you can exercise skills and imagination at any

time, regardless of whether you are currently in a play. You may find parts of this book strike you as relevant to your life and work, while other parts feel more distant. Do not dismiss any part out of hand, but allow yourself to practice and strengthen the skills: both the ones that come naturally and the ones that feel more awkward to you. Revisit this book from time to time, as you may find that when you are in a different place, the methodology speaks to you differently.

Thank you for spending time with this book.

appendix A

ACTION WORD LEXICON

The following lexicon is provided for you as a resource. You can refer to this list when choosing actions for roles you are rehearsing, monologues and soliloquies you are preparing for audition, classroom work and practice on your own or with a friend. Some choices will work for some actors, while others will not. The only way you will know if an action works for you is to choose it, work with it, and see what you discover. As it is by no means comprehensive, this need not be a static document, but one that you can add to whenever you come across an action that works for you. In this way it becomes a private tool. In using it, recall how to phrase your action choices. For example, *I want to make him/her/it feel loved.* Substitute any word from the list for "loved" in considering whether or not to use it.

A
adored
afraid
amused
angry
annoyed
anxious
ashamed
at ease
at attention
attentive

B
bad
beautiful
bewitched

badgered
battered
beaten
belittled

C
calm
capable
cared for
challenged
charmed
cheap
cheerful
cherished
comfortable
conceited

confident
confronted
contemtable
controlled
cool
cornered
creepy
criticized
cruel
crushed
cunning
curious

D
dangerous
dared

dazzled
deceitful
degraded
delighted
deserving
disgusting
dismissed
dominated
doomed
dull

E
ecstatic
elated
encouraged
energized
enraged
entertained
envious
excited
exhilerated
exposed

F
fear
feeble
feminine
foolish
forgiven
frazzled
freakish
free
frivolous
frustrated
furious

G
glad
gratified

greedy
guilty

H
happy
harmless
hated
hopeful
hopeless
horrible
horrified
hot
humble
humiliated
hurried
hysterical

I
idiotic
idolized
ignorant
ignored
immature
imperfect
important
impotent
incompetent
inept
inferior
insecure
insignificant
interesting
intimidated
invited
irrelevant
irresponsible

J
jealous

jubilant

L
lazy
light
lonely
loved
low
lowesome
lusty

M
mad
majestic
manly
mistaken
mocked
mortified
mothered
motivated
mysterious

N
nagged
nasty
naughty
nauseated
needed
needled
nervous
normal
nostalgic
nosy
nourished
numbly

O
odd
offended

on-the-spot
optimistic
outraged
overwhelmed

P
panic
paranoia
pathetic
peaceful
perturbed
phony
pious
pitiful
playful
pompous
positive
possessed
potent
powerful
powerless
precious
preferred
pretentious
prophetic
protected
proud
pushed

R
radiant
reassured
regal
regretful
rejected

remorseful
resented
ridiculous
rotten

S
sad
safe
satiated
satisfied
sentimental
serene
servile
sexy
shaken
shocked
shunned
silly
sinful
slimey
sly
small
soothed
sorry
special
spited
still
strange
strapping
strong
stubborn
snobby
stupid
superior
surprised

suspected
sweet
sympathetic

T
tamed
teased
tempted
tested
thanked
threatened
trapped
trusted
turned-on

U
upset
useless

V
valued
vindicated
violated

W
wanted
warned
weird
welcome
worried
worthless
worthy
wrong

HOW OF THE ACTION WORD LEXICON

The following lexicon is provided for you as a resource. Refer to this list when choosing the *how* of the action for your action choices, but also to help you to consider the ways in which your *Who am I?* might be expressed based on your examination of the play. As with action choices, some choices for the how of the action will work for some actors, while other choices will not; some will seem appropriate for the *Who am I?*, while others will not. Often the how of your action as the character will spring naturally as a response to the how of the action from another actor as character in a scene with you. For example, if an actor as a character is attempting to make you as a character feel stupid *aggressively* (or *in an aggressive way*), you as the character may make him feel wrong *defensively* (or *in a defensive way*). Your how of the action is in response to his how of the action. Said in another way, your defensiveness is in response to his aggressiveness. However, sometimes you will want to make other choices. The only way that you will know if a choice works for you is to work with it to see what you discover. Like the action lexicon, as this is by no means a comprehensive list, it need not be a static document, but one you can add to whenever you come across a how of the action that works for you. In this way it becomes a private tool. In using it, recall how to phrase your action choices. For example, *I want to make him/her/it feel loved*. The *how* of the action is the way in which the action is played. For example, *I want to make him/her/it feel loved tenderly* (or *in a tender way*).

A	amorous	arrogant
abnormal	animalistic	assertive
affectionate	anti-social	
aggressive	anxious	**B**
aloof	apologetic	bitter

blissful
bloodthirsty
boorish
bossy
brave
brazen
brotherly
brutal
bubbly
bullying

C
callous
calm
caring
cautious
charming
cheerful
cold
cold-blooded
compulsive
conceited
confident
confrontational
contemtuous
controlling
coy
crabby
cranky
crazy
creepy
crestfallen
critical
cruel
cunning
curt
cynical

D
daring

decisive
defensive
deflated
delicate
desperate
disappointed
disgruntled
disgusted
dismissive
distant
distraught
docile
dominating
dorky

E
eager
easy
ecstatic
elegant
energetic
entertaining
enthusiatic
exasperated
excited
exhausted
expectant

F
fatherly
feeble
fiendish
fierce
flippant
flirtacious
forceful
frank
frantic
frazzled
freakish

frenzied
frivolous
frustrated
fussy

G
geeky
generous
gentle
glamorous
glum
grateful
greedy
gruff
grumpy
guarded

H
haphazard
hateful
heartless
helpful
helpless
hesitant
hopeful
hopeless
hostile
humble
hysterical

I
icy
idiotic
immature
impatient
impulsive
indifferent
inquisitive
insecure
intimidating
irksome

ironical

J
jealous
joking
jovial
jubilant
jumpy

K
kind
kinky

L
lackluster
lanquid
lazy
light
listless
loopy
loquacious
loving
lustful

M
majestic
maniacle
manly
mean
meek
merciful
mocking
morbid
morose
motherly
mysterious

N
nagging
nasty

needy
negative
nervous
nostalgic
nosy
numb

O
obsessive
offensive
open
optimistic

P
panicked
paranoid
passionate
passive
pathetic
peaceful
pensive
pessimistic
phony
picky
pious
playful
polite
pompous
positive
powerful
powerless
praising
pretentious
prophetic
protective
proud
pushy

Q
quarrelsome

questioning
quick
quirky

R
radiant
raging
rambunctious
reckless
regal
regretful
remorseful
resentful
reserved
resigned
resistent
reticent
reverent
romantic
royal

S
sarcastic
satisfied
savage
scolding
scornful
seductive
self-loathing
self-pitying
sensual
sentimental
serene
servile
sexy
shifty
sisterly
skeptical
slow
sly

snobby

soft

soothing

sorrowful

sparkling

spiteful

spoiled

stern

still

strong

submissive

subtle

superior

suspicious

sweet

sympathetic

T

timid

tempting

testing

threatening

U

uncertain

uptight

V

violent

W

weary

weird

welcoming

whiney

wishy washy

ANNOTATIONS FOR PLAYS MENTIONED IN THIS BOOK

Albee, Edward: *Who's Afraid of Virginia Woolf*

This play won a Tony and a New York Drama Critics' Circle award when it was first produced in the early 1960s. Sharp-tongued Martha is married to quiet college professor George. When they invite a younger couple over one evening, a night of hard-drinking leads to painful confrontations and degenerates into the bitter death of an imaginary child. This play offers actors many opportunities to explore subtext, for practice in creating objectives that are not obviously contained in the spoken lines themselves.

Albee, Edward: *The Zoo Story*

Edward Albee's first play, first produced in 1960, is set in a single location: a park bench in Central Park. Most of the play is conversation, with a violently physical ending. Jerry, sloppily dressed and a bit gone to seed, engages Peter (somewhat against Peter's will) in conversation one sunny afternoon. As both players are on stage throughout the play, *The Zoo Story* offers the opportunity for actors to explore transitioning from objective to objective while remaining an active part of the scene on stage.

Beckett, Samuel: *Endgame*

Hamm, Clov, Nagg, and Nell inhabit a small room in a gray world, participating in conversations that sometimes appear to border on the nonsensical. Two of the characters don't have legs and make their occasional appearances from trashcans. Hamm plays his part from a chair, while Clov is never seated. Hamm and Clov are in constant push-pull of staying and leaving, and many of the conversations border on the ridiculous, in keeping with the style dubbed "theatre of the absurd." In playing Nagg or Nell (and to a lesser extent, Clov and Hamm), an actor has the chance to explore a role with severe physical/movement constraints.

Beckett, Samuel: *Waiting for Godot*

Probably the best know of plays in the style known as theatre of the absurd, *Waiting for Godot* has all the hallmarks of absurdist theater: illogical, disharmonious, ridiculous in its conclusions, and often bizarre. This play has little plot, little setting, and little background for the characters. It appears to be about . . . nothing. Vladimir and Estragon, usually portrayed as disheveled tramps, along with Pozzo, Lucky and a boy have various disjointed conversations and make their entrances and exits, all the while waiting for a key player who never appears. The play offers abundant opportunity to explore creating objectives and playing actions in a nonlinear play.

Brecht, Bertolt: *Mother Courage and Her Children*

Sometimes shortened to the title *Mother Courage*, this highly charged antiwar political drama, was written in the midst of World War II, but is set in the 1700s. Mother Courage ekes out a living by selling provisions to soldiers from her cart, even as the lives her children are claimed by the war. The play offers ample opportunity to explore stereotypes and direct-address.

Chekhov, Anton: *Ivanov*

Ivanov is the bleak story of a man beset by depression. He was once excited about life, with plans to better himself and the world, and he was married to the woman he loved. Now, he is heavily in debt and spends his days away from home. His wife, who still loves him, catches him in a kiss with another woman. His wife then dies of tuberculosis, and although Ivanov and Sasha (the "other woman") make plans to marry, Ivanov does not follow through and instead kills himself off stage at the end of the play. The play offers ample opportunity to explore the *Who am I?* informed by resignation, depression, and despair.

Chekhov, Anton: *The Sea Gull*

Treplev, a frustrated playwright, loves Nina, who wants to be an actress. Nina used to love Treplev fully, but now finds her head turned by Trigorin, a famous actor, who is romantically partnered with Treplev's mother as the play opens. The play in general, and one scene in particular, is given a detailed exploration in chapter five.

Chekhov, Anton: *The Three Sisters*

Three sisters and their brother live in a small town, away from Moscow. The sisters look forward to small brightness in their days, such as the visits from army officers stationed nearby. When Andre begins courting Natasha, a young woman from the town, the sisters are surprised, but they never think he would marry her. When Act II begins, Andre and Natasha are married, and have a son, thus changing the family dynamic and the lives of Olga, Masha, and Irina. This play is rich in opportunity to explore the *Who am I?* strongly informed by relationships.

Chekhov, Anton: *The Cherry Orchard*

Madame Ranevskaya returns to her family's land after a five-year absence. Payments on the mortgage are far behind, but she refuses to consider suggestions for raising the money. Lopakhin, a former serf who Madame nurtured as a youth has risen to the level of businessman, and Varya, Madame Ranevskaya's adopted daughter, hopes that he may propose. In the end, the cherry orchard is purchases by Lopakhin, who is pleased to be the owner of the land where once he toiled. He cuts down the cherry trees in order to build estates that he will sell to pay the mortgage. The play offers ample opportunity to explore how changing circumstances affect the *Who am I?*, the *Where am I?*, and the *When am I there?*

Chekhov, Anton: *Uncle Vanya*

Uncle Ivan (called by the nickname Vanya) is a weary man, who has worked much of his life for his brother-in-law Serabryakov on Serabryakov's estate. Serabryakov has a number of ailments and calls often upon Astrov, a conscientious doctor from the town. Yelena, Serabryakov's younger second wife has fallen in love with the doctor, as has Sonya, Serabryakov's daughter from his first marriage. Vanya is in love with Yelena, and eventually attempts to shoot the professor, though he misses with both shots. Serebryakov and Yelena depart the estate, as does Astrov. Sonya (the daughter from the first marriage) and Vanya return to their quiet lives. This play is rich in opportunity to explore super-objectives that are never achieved and the relationships of the *Who am I?*. One particularly interesting exploration is *Who am I?* (when I am with you) between Yelena and her stepdaughter Sonya, who is almost the same age and in love with the same man.

Frayn, Michael: *Copenhagen*

Although Frayn may be better known for *Noises Off*, his elaborate front stage/back stage comedy demands not one but two elaborate and carefully constructed sets with many specific props, *Copenhagen* is an equally demanding work, in a very different way. There are three actors (all of whom are dead during the play), remembering (and perhaps mis-remembering) events in the past. The play has the sparest of sets, with long monologues heavy on scientific jargon, and yet the three actors keep circling back to key questions of morality and humanity. As *Copenhagen* is based on historical characters and events, there is opportunity to use historical research to enrich the exploration of *Who am I?*.

Gibson, William: *The Miracle Worker*

First produced in 1959, this play has strong roles for a younger woman (pre-teen Helen Keller) and her tutor Annie Sullivan, in her early 20s. The play features a number of surrounding family members and subplots, but the main focus is on Helen and Annie, as Annie struggles (often quite physically) to open the door for Helen to step into the universe of those who see, hear, and speak. As Helen has no lines in the play, although she has many chances at primitive vocalizations, this play offers the opportunity to transform into a *Who am I?* with distinct physical challenges. The role of Annie also offers physical transformation as she is not a physically imposing person, but she must battle with Helen in the play.

Hansberry, Lorraine: *A Raisin in the Sun*

Hansberry's 1959 play, winner of the New York Drama Critics' Circle Award, was the first play by a black woman to be produced on Broadway. The play is set in a downtrodden area of Chicago, in the "present day" of the playwright. It looks at members of the extended Younger family as they contemplate the "best" way to spend $10,000 from a life insurance policy. The play offers ample opportunity to explore *Who am I?*, *Where am I?*, and *When am I there?* as the play deals with race and class and the narratives surrounding being dark-skinned in a society and at a time when lighter skin was often perceived as "better."

Ibsen, Henrik: *A Doll House*

One of Ibsen's best-known plays (sometimes translated as *A Doll's House*) has a strong current of feminism as well as a rich psychological component. The role of Nora offers a great opportunity to explore the evolution of the *Who am I?*.

Ibsen, Henrik: *The Enemy of the People*

Written a few years after *A Doll's House*, this play pits two brothers against one another: Dr. Thomas Stockmann, who finds the town's water is contaminated, and his brother, a town leader, who would like to keep the baths open for the financial good of the town. *The Enemy of the People* offers opportunity to explore how sociopolitical views inform the *Who am I?*.

Ibsen, Henrik: *Hedda Gabler*

Hedda Gabler (who isn't best known by her married name of Tesman, though women at that time were clearly expected to be identified through their husband) tries to manipulate events out of her own jealously and in an attempt to benefit her husband's career. Hedda is an overbearing character, yet one who also appreciates beauty in life. Ibsen adds challenge for the actor portraying Hedda, as her method for getting what she wants tends to be seen as unsympathetic. This play offers challenging opportunities to explore *What do I want?*.

Mamet, David: *Race*

Race delivers strong language, blunt phrases, and topics not spoken of among polite folk in society. *Race* has four characters: a white lawyer, a black lawyer, a new legal team member (young, black and female), and the rich white man they must defend against the charge of raping a black woman. This play has Mamet's rhythmic fast-paced language, four letter words, and several plot twists packed into its two-act. The play offers the opportunity to explore sociopolitical views and how they inform the *Who am I?*.

McDonagh, Martin: *The Pillowman*

An Olivier award winner in 2004, this dark play from Irish playwright Martin McDonagh is layered with reality that loops back on itself and on the storytelling within the play. Katurian has been arrested and a bad cop/worse cop team is holding his mentally challenged brother hostage in a neighboring room. They are determined to wring from Katurian a confession to child murders that bear an eerie resemblance to his short stories. The play offers ample opportunity to explore seeing the world from the point of view of the *Who am I?*.

McPherson, Conor: *The Weir*

The Weir, winner of the 1999 Olivier award from the Society of London, is set in that "present day," on a wet and windy night in the Irish countryside. Four long-time acquaintances (one cannot quite call them friends) meet as usual in a somewhat seedy local pub, on the edge of the moors. On this particular evening, a newcomer, Valerie, has stepped into the pub, causing the usual alignment among the men to be thrown off. The play progresses largely through monologues as the four men tell ghost stories to Valerie, the audience, and to each other, and then Valerie tells one, herself. The play provides challenging opportunities to apply the questions *What do I want?* and *How do I get it?* to characters that tell stories.

Miller, Arthur: *The Crucible*

This play offers several strong roles for women. The play concerns accusations of witchcraft made under questionable circumstances against the townsfolk of Salem. The specific historic setting (Salem, Massachusetts, 1692) offers a solid foothold for researching and creating a detailed *Who am I?, Where am I?,* and *When am I there?.*

Shepard, Sam: *Fool for Love*

Fool for Love shows Eddie and May, a can't live with 'em, can't live without 'em couple, alternately embracing and at each other's throats. Eddie and May (and the audience) can see and hear The Old Man, who doesn't exist in the real life of the play, but as a father figure to both characters. The play offers ample opportunity to explore *Who am I?* in richly drawn characters.

Shepard, Sam: *Savage/Love*

This performance piece is one of several collaborations by this pair in the space of about seven years. *Savage/Love* is spare and bare, almost poetic, and is meant to be accompanied by music and film or video. The characters meet and fall in love, but instead of "happily ever after" they grow further apart. The short bursts of dialogue allow actors ample opportunity to explore many action choices.

Stetson, Jeff: *The Meeting*

In this one-act play, Stetson shows an imagined clandestine meeting between Dr. Martin Luther King Jr. and Malcolm X in a room in a Harlem hotel. Stetson's play has been praised for his thoughtful recreation of each speaker's natural speaking style, and the play uses words and phrases that each man actually spoke, along with imagined dialogue. The play offers the opportunity for transformation into a *Who am I?* based on a real person.

Strindberg, August: *Miss Julie*

Strindberg, a Swedish playwright, published *Miss Julie* in 1888. It was considered shocking at that time and immediately censored for out rightly stating the idea that sex could be separate from love. Miss Julie, a wealthy daughter disregards class lines and has an affair with Jean, her father's valet. This play offers opportunities to explore status and social class and how they affect the *Who am I?* and *Who am I? when I am with you.*

Strindberg, August: *The Ghost Sonata*

Swedish playwright August Strindberg was never afraid to experiment, and his plays, written over about 40 years, embrace the trends of naturalism, realism, modernism, and the use of psychology and spirituality (among other trends). *The Ghost Sonata* is one of his "chamber plays," created for a small theater with which Strindberg was involved in the early 1900s. The plays include a small cast, minimal sets and often do not adhere to reality. Events in *The Ghost Sonata* are not linear, and the setting is an imaginary, dream-like place. Strindberg used the intimate theatre space to experiment with sparse sets, colored lights for atmosphere, and seemingly modern ideas such as projected images of scenery. Although some of the characters in the *Ghost Sonata* have names, they are also identified through labels such as "The Old Man" "The Colonel" 'The Mummy" and "The Milkmaid." *The Ghost Sonata* offers the chance to explore how spirituality informs the *Who am I?* and also offers opportunities to explore physical transformation.

Williams, Tennessee: *Cat on a Hot Tin Roof*

Brick, a hard-drinking high school athlete past his prime and Maggie, his scheming and frustrated wife, are two major roles in Williams' Pulitzer Prize winning play from 1955. Maggie is concerned that without a child, she and Brick may find themselves without an inheritance when Big Daddy dies. The play offers challenging opportunity to explore subtext.

Williams, Tennessee: *Eccentricities of a Nightingale*

Set in the deep south of Glorious Hill, Mississippi, *Eccentricities of a Nightingale* tells the story of Alma, a mentally fragile woman and her obsession with her love for Dr. Buchanan, who isn't a bad fellow at heart, even as his mother tries to break up any thought of romance. With its specific, deep-south setting, this play offers the opportunity to explore a dialect as a part of *Who am I?* as well as a chance to explore mentally disturbed characters.

Williams, Tennessee: *A Streetcar Named Desire*

Awarded a Pulitzer Prize and the New York Drama Critics' Circle Award, Williams' well-known play is set in French Quarter of New Orleans. Family relationships are pivotal in this play, with mounting tensions as Stella and her husband Stanley adjust when Stella's sister Blanche moves in. This play offers the actor as Blanche many opportunities to practice using her imagination to create sources not present on stage, as she is portrayed as generally living in a world of her making to the point where she is disbelieved when she tells the truth about Stanley's attack. The play offers opportunity to explore how *Where am I from?* and *Where am I now?* collide and inform the *Who am I?*

The Works of William Shakespeare

Shakespeare's writings offer the opportunity to explore almost every conceivable human condition. Love, hate, trickery, treachery, evil, witchcraft, madness, bravery, humor . . . it is all in one play or sonnet or another. Among other things, there is ample opportunity to explore how the Elizabethan worldview informs the *Who am I?*.

Hamlet

Hamlet is one of the best known and most frequently produced of Shakespeare's plays. Often it is performed in an abridged format, but still requires a great deal of costuming and scenery. Hamlet's father dies and his mother quickly remarries Hamlet's uncle, the new king, much to Hamlet's distress and dismay.

Henry V

Henry V is the center of this history play, which has a large cast of mostly men and can be expanded to almost any size on stage with the addition of lords, ladies, courtiers, attendants, soldiers, and townspeople. Henry is portrayed as a brave and worthy man, both on and off the battlefield. He marries Katherine, daughter of the King of France thus gaining control of that country as well. His patriotic and moving speeches include one to his soldiers (whom he has visited in disguise) that they are a "band of brothers"—a family—and that their valiant deeds will never be forgotten.

Henry VI Part 1

The first of three history plays on the life of Henry VI, this first play follows the younger life of Henry VI and his rise to king. Joan La Pucelle (Joan of Arc) has a significant part in this play, leading men into battle and fighting on behalf of France until she is captured near the end of the play and ordered to burn at the stake. The first play takes him from his early years to young adulthood.

Macbeth

Power and the getting thereof is one of the major themes in *Macbeth*. Macbeth devises a plot with his wife to kill King Duncan to take over the Scottish throne. Three witches have made prophesies to various people in the play, and one by one the prophesies come true. Eventually Lady Macbeth's guilty conscience gets the better of her, and she kills herself. Macbeth is killed in battle.

Measure for Measure

Measure for Measure looks at corruption and immorality, along with mercy, in this dark comedy. Angelo, appointed ruler of Vienna in the Duke's absence, vows to clean up the city and put an end to prostitution. He arrests Claudio, whose fiancée is pregnant, but later strikes an immoral deal of his own with Claudio's sister. In the end, Isabella maintains her chastity, and Claudio is set free.

A Midsummer Night's Dream

The passions in this play are numerous. Hermia loves Lysander, but her father is insisting she marry Demetrius. Demetrius loves Hermia, but not long ago he preferred Helena. Helena still loves Demetrius. In the forest, where the four young people escape, they encounter magic, which turns their world topsy-turvy until Puck makes it right in the end. In other plots, the fairy King and Queen, Oberon and Titania, are quarreling, and a group of amateur actors are practicing a play to present to the Duke at his wedding.

Much Ado About Nothing

Much Ado about Nothing is set on a luxurious estate in Messina, Italy, with an elegant villa and grounds. A prince and his officers pay a lengthy visit to Leonato, the mayor of Messina, who lives with his only daughter, Hero. Hero's cousin Beatrice is a witty young woman who scorns love and often crosses verbal swords with Benedick, a young man from nearby. Leonato's brother Don Joun hatches a scheme to break up the happy couple of Hero and a soldier, Claudius, while the townspeople jokingly push together the avowed singles, Beatrice and Benedick. A hapless village constable and his cronies take center stage from time to time, usually to great amusement.

Othello

Othello is steeped in tragedy and deceit. Othello, a commander, promotes Cassio rather than Iago, and Iago sets out for revenge. He stirs up trouble between Desdemona and her father, and orchestrates Cassio's demotion. His most destructive lies concern a supposed affair between Desdemona and Cassio. Othello cruelly berates Desdemona in his jealous rage. Iago's wife Emelia is Desdemona's servant and also her bosom friend. She introduces a conversation that explores infidelity and violence. Othello strangles Desdemona in the end, while Iago kills Emelia. Othello than kills himself, while Iago is led off to be punished.

Richard III

This largely male cast nonetheless has meaty roles for women in Queen Elizabeth, Margaret, and Lady Ann. Richard III wants the crown currently held by his brother and is willing to do what he deems necessary to get it. He murders another brother and locks two princes in a tower, where they perish. He turns on Lord Hastings, and others who get in his way are killed as well. Richard is slain on the battlefield by Henry, Duke of Richmond, who then assumes the crown as King Henry VII.

Romeo and Juliet

"In fair Verona, where we lay our scene. . . ." The houses of Capulet and Montague are feuding, and the star-crossed lovers, Romeo and Juliet, meet, court, marry, and die. This most classic of tragedies follows the two young people and their households, and the long-standing feud is ultimately ended by the deaths of Romeo and Juliet.

The Tempest

Prospero has been purposefully cast away on a mostly deserted island with his teenage daughter, Miranda. The island is inhabited by various sprites, led by Ariel, and Caliban, a deformed monster who is in love with Miranda. Prospero has learned how to work magic on the island, and he causes a storm that strands a ship and deposits his brother, along with the crew, on the island. Caliban in particular is a physically challenging role, and he is usually portrayed as being deformed in shape and movement and sometimes voice as well. Other actors play scenes in various states of drunkenness. Some of the sprites take the shape of "dogs and hounds" in Act IV

The Two Gentlemen of Verona

Valentine and Proteus are the gentlemen in question, both of whom fall for Silvia, daughter of the Duke of Milan. The Duke prefers that Silvia marry Thurio, though Silvia herself loves Valentine. She spurns Proteus, pointing out that until recently, he had loved Julia. Jealous Proteus reveals Valentine's plans to elope with Silvia, resulting in Valentine's banishment. Soon Julia arrives in Milan, dressed as a boy. Silvia goes into the forest to rescue Valentine, who was captured by outlaws. Proteus follows Silvia, the disguised Julia follows Proteus and by the end, the couples Silvia and Valentine and Julia and Proteus have sorted themselves out and plan to share wedding day.

The Winter's Tale

The Winter's Tale is driven in great part by the jealously of King Leontes toward his wife and Polixenes, an old friend. There are interesting explorations of status, as King Leontes banishes his baby daughter, who he wrongly believes to have been fathered by Polixenes. The girl is found on a beach and raised by a shepherd. At the beginning of Act IV, a chorus appears, representing time, and announces that "o'er sixteen years" has slid by, as if the audience had slept. Polixenes son, not knowing the now-grown shepherd girl's true heritage, falls in love with her to his father's displeasure. Luckily, a box of keepsakes is produced, which proves that Perdita is not lowborn, but in fact the daughter of the king. Polixenes gives his blessing that they marry. This play winds up rather well, with the young couple united and general repentance and forgiveness all around.

Works Cited

Albee, Edward. *The American Dream and Zoo Story*. New York: Plume-Penguin, 1997.

Beckett, Samuel. *Endgame*. New York: Grove Press, 1958.

---. Waiting for Godot. New York: Grove Press, 1954.

Chekhov, Michael. *To the Author*. New York: Routledge, 1983.

Chekhov, Anton. "The Cherry Orchard." *Six Plays of Chekhov*. Edited by Robert Corrigan. New York: Holt, Rinehart and Winston, 1962.

---. "The Seagull." *Six Plays of Chekhov*. Edited by Robert Corrigan. New York: Holt, Rinehart and Winston, 1962.

---. "The Three Sisters." *Six Plays of Chekhov*. Edited by Robert Corrigan. New York: Holt, Rinehart and Winston, 1962.

---. "Uncle Vanya." *Six Plays of Chekhov*. Edited by Robert Corrigan. New York: Holt, Rinehart and Winston, 1962.

Hornby, Richard. *The End of Acting*. New York: Applause, 1993.

Ibsen, Henrik. *A Doll House*. New York: Dover, 1990.

Magarshack, David. *Chekhov the Dramatist*. New York: Hill and Wang, 1960.

Miller, Arthur. *The Crucible*. New York: Penguin, 1952.

Playbill.com. "Earle Gister, Yale Acting Master, Stages His Passion, *The Sea Gull*, in NYC, May 24-29." Accessed October 17, 2011. http://www.playbill.com/news/article/86319-Earle-Gister-Yale-Acting-Master-Stages-His-Passion-The-Seagull-in-NYC-May-24-29

Shepard, Sam. *Fool for Love and Other Plays*. New York: Bantam Books, 1983

Strindberg, August. "The Ghost Sonata." In *Selected Plays*. Translated by Evert Sprinchorn. Minneapolis: Univ. of Minnesota Press, 1986.

Shakespeare, William. *The Riverside Shakespeare*. Edited by G. Blakemore Evans and J.J.M. Tobin. New York: Houghton Mifflin, 1997.

Acting: The Gister Method (Alberti) Index